VISIONS OF REALITY

Religion and Ethnicity in Social Work

Edited by Naina Patel, Don Naik and Beth Humphries

CCETSW✓

**Central Council for
Education and Training
in Social Work**

Published by:
Central Council for Education
and Training in Social Work,
Derbyshire House, St. Chad's Street,
London WC1H 8AD

© Central Council for Education and
Training in Social Work 1998

First published March 1998

ISBN 1 85719 181 1

CCETSW is a registered charity.

Designed by:
Sign

Cover design:
Hot Frog Graphics

Printed by:
Latimer Trend

The extracts from the Runnymede Commission's report
*A Very Light Sleeper – the Persistence and Dangers of
Antisemitism* on pp 69-73 are reprinted with kind
permission of the Chief Executive of the Runnymede Trust

"Religion and Social Work – it's not that simple!" by Paul
Sanzenbach (with responses by Edward R Canda and
M. Vincentia Joseph) on pp 84-92 is reprinted from *Social
Casework: The Journal of Contemporary Social Work*,
published by Families International, Inc, November 1989

"Crossing the Divide" by Reba Bhaduri on pp 93-96 is
reprinted from *Social Work Today* 29 March 1990 and
published by permission of the Editor of *Community Care*

"Overcoming Abuse: An Islamic Approach" by Aliya Haeri on
pp 97-101 is © 1994 *OpenMind* and reprinted from
OpenMind 69, June/July 1994 by permission of MIND
(National Association for Mental Health)

"Social Work, Sectarianism and Anti-Sectarian Practice in
Northern Ireland" by Marie Smyth and Jim Campbell on
pp 102-115 is reprinted from *British Journal of Social Work*,
1996, Volume 26, pp 77-92

The views expressed in this publication
are those of the authors and do not
necessarily reflect those of CCETSW.

A message from the Minister

In our multi-cultural, multi-faith society, it is important to the strategic planning, care management and service delivery processes for social care managers and practitioners to appreciate the importance of religion and faith to people's lives and values.

Those who provide and receive social work training and education will find many useful messages in the essays and readings of this book. Appreciation of these messages can lead to more appropriate and non-discriminatory social care practices and services.

Paul Boateng MP
Parliamentary Under Secretary of State, Department of Health

Contents

Foreword i
Preface ii
Notes on contributors iv
Acknowledgements v

Part 1: Understanding religion and ethnicity in social work
Chapter 1   Introduction *by Naina Patel, Don Naik and Beth Humphries*   2
Chapter 2   Ethnic minorities and religious affiliations: their size and impact on
            social work *by Kaushika Amin*   20
Chapter 3   The case for religion in social work education: an independent
            view of social work and ethnicity *by Sunita Thakur*   42

Part 2: Case studies of religion and ethnicity in social work practice
Chapter 4   The AWWAZ group   52
Chapter 5   Jewish issues in social work education: 69
            Section 1: The dimensions of antisemitism
            by the Runnymede Commission on Antisemitism, the Runnymede Trust   69
            Section 2: Practice issues *by Jennifer Wood*   74
Chapter 6   Reprints of four articles: 84
            – Religion and social work: it's not that simple! (1989)
              *by Paul Sanzenbach (with responses by Edward R. Canda
              and M. Vincentia Joseph)*   84
            – Crossing the divide (1990) *by Reba Bhaduri*   93
            – Overcoming abuse: an Islamic approach (1994) *by Aliya Haeri*   97
            – Social work, sectarianism and anti-sectarian practice in
              Northern Ireland (1996) *by Marie Smyth and Jim Campbell*   102

Part 3: Directory and bibliographies
Chapter 7   Religious faith and communities: directory and select
            bibliographies for social workers *by Kaushika Amin*   120

Other publications from CCETSW   156

Foreword

There are some 1,250,000 people engaged in social work and social care activities in the UK. NISW (1995) research demonstrated that they are highly committed and become distressed when through lack of training or resources they are unable to respond adequately to service users' needs. Among these staff will be those who practise a particular religion and those who do not. Such diversity may be reflected among service users, from majority and minority groups.

This book's starting point is that religion and religious thoughts and practices are integral to people's lives. In working in a multi-racial, multi-faith society, social work and social care staff facing diverse needs and values have to take decisions and act upon them. As Professor David Weir* says in *Business Ethics, the Religious Dimension*: "The core of management practices is the exercise of trained judgement... Good judgements are based on an implicit structure of ethical precepts." Social workers' decisions and judgements are similarly informed by their training, competence and the values they hold.

In CCETSW's Equal Opportunities Policy Statement** agreed in 1995 and incorporated in the rules and requirements for its awards and schemes, service users' religious beliefs and values are regarded as being a part of social work values. The significance attached to religion is also reflected in the Children Act 1989 and the NHS and Community Care Act 1990.

The co-editors have therefore brought together in a three-part structure a comprehensive collection of essays and selected readings to help in the social care and social work task of "trained judgement". They have recognised the differing aspects of religious practices and discrimination on the grounds of religion in the UK and examined anti-semitism and sectarianism. The selection is primarily designed to assist students, candidates and trainers to meet CCETSW's requirements. Given that care and welfare extends beyond social work and that religious and minority issues extend beyond the geographical boundaries of the UK, much in this book will be relevant to those working in related fields and in Europe.

The book is also timely, being one of CCETSW's contributions to the European Year Against Racism, Xenophobia and Anti-Semitism 1997. I hope that it will be thoughtfully read by those involved in improving education and services to our multi-racial and multi-faith societies.

Liz Wulff-Cochrane
Head of Development and Promotions Department, CCETSW, London

---

* Weir, D. (1997) *Business Ethics, the Religious Dimension*, in Marshell, E. (ed.) *Working Paper No 9705*, The Management Centre, University of Braford
** CCETSW (1996) *Equal Opportunities Policy Statement*

Preface

Everyone is influenced by religion and religious practices whether they are believers, agnostics or atheists. Social service users are no exception. Yet religious cultural practices, group and individual spirituality, religious divisions and religion as therapy have had no place in social work education and practice even though social work has its origins in religious philanthropy. Ever the invisible presence in modern social work, its place should be recognised and taken account of in the work of the profession.

This book aims to contribute to the debate on the role of belief in the lives of service users, students, practitioners and tutors. It is timely as Britain has a complex mix of both organised and alternative religions about which negative stereotypes abound, sometimes influenced by racism.

One of a range of publications on equal opportunities from CCETSW, it should be read alongside the complementary training pack *Children, Spirituality and Religion*. Neither publication is an encyclopaedia of religion nor a checklist of beliefs which can be found in publications from each of the religions referred to. Rather they offer resources to social work educators and practitioners to enable them to understand better the influence of religion on the lives of service users.

Visions of Reality is also part of a wider project – the promotion of equal opportunities and antiracism in social work. It brings a neglected perspective to debates about racism and focuses on the dilemmas often faced by social workers arising from the religious beliefs of service users.

Contributors have not avoided difficult issues which, as editors, we are aware may stir people's sensitivities about their religious beliefs and racial identity. Touch religion and you touch a person's deepest being. However, use of the term "ethnicity" has enabled us to range widely to include experiences of groups such as Jewish and Irish people whose ethnicity and religion are intimately entwined but who might have been excluded by some definitions of race.

Structure
The three chapters in Part 1 "Understanding Religion and Ethnicity in Social Work" provide a foundation, within an equal opportunities and antiracist framework, for readers to understand how religion, religious thought and practices in whatever form are integral to people's lives.

Part 2 comprises original and already published case studies of how religion and ethnicity can affect social work practice – experiences of an Asian women's group; anti-Semitism; the role of religion in social work values; bereavement counselling; an Islamic approach to child abuse; and sectarianism.

Part 3 "Directory and Bibliographies" is a guide for readers seeking to become better informed on a particular religion or specific aspects of it.

We hope this book will be a useful addition to the social work literature and help in the training of social workers to practice effectively in our multiracial and multi-faith society.

Naina Patel
Don Naik
Beth Humphries
August 1997

Notes on contributors

Kaushika Amin is the editor of *Runnymede Bulletin*, a newsletter of the Runnymede Trust which is an independent charity concerned with issues of racial justice and equality. She has worked on several of the trust's national projects and produced its reports. She is the co-author of *Poverty and Race in Britain* and co-editor of *Growing Old Far From Home*.

Beth Humphries is Research Degrees Co-ordinator at the Department of Applied Community Studies at Manchester Metropolitan University. She recently edited *Critical Perspectives on Empowerment* and co-authored CCETSW's CD Project publication, *Practice Teaching*, seventh in the Antiracist Social Work Education series.

Don Naik is a consultant and external assessor in social work and has worked on projects with the United Nations in South Africa and Cambodia. He was formerly the Assistant Dean of the Faculty of Environment and Social Studies at the University of North London, a CCETSW Council member and the Chair of the Council's Black Perspectives Committee.

Naina Patel is a project manager at CCETSW covering Equal Opportunities and Europe. She also works for CNEOPSA – a transnational project on managing care in dementia for minority ethnic older people based at the Management Centre, University of Bradford.

Sunita Thakur is a journalist, currently based in India. She contributes to various BBC radio programmes, including *Woman's Hour* in the UK. She previously worked at Radio Leeds.

Jennifer Wood has a background in mental health work and was an Approved Social Worker. She has worked as a training officer in social services and recently as a training co-ordinator and practice teacher at Manchester Jewish Federation. She is currently a lecturer in social work at Salford University.

NB: *Contributors of articles reprinted in Chapter 6 are referred to in the text.*

Acknowledgements

This book had considerable support from CCETSW's Equal Opportunities Consultative Group, in particular Dorothy Neoh, Gill Michael, Alexandra Seale, Gillian Loughran, Andy Stevens, Aled Jones, Paul Hicks and Gamaledin M. Ashami who discussed the issues with us and provided papers. Thanks are also due to Alison Harris, Abena Asantewa and Abi Okedji for assistance with the search for articles and administration; to Jessie Bura for typing the selected printed articles and the text, and to Dipesh Patel for proof-reading. Thanks also to the many individuals – Shuchi Bhatt, Agnes Martin and Hansa Chouhan in particular – who took an interest in the project and encouraged us to complete it.

We are most grateful to Hafiz R. Mirza for creating an appropriate title for this book.

Our thanks and acknowledgement also to the editors and publishers for giving copyright permission to reprint the articles reproduced in Chapter 6.

We would like to pay particular tribute to George Smith (CCETSW 1972-97) who as CCETSW's Editorial Adviser made helpful comments and suggested revisions to the text of this book and, sadly, died during the course of its production. George worked with us closely for over a decade on CCETSW's previous antiracist/equal opportunities publications.

We would also like to thank Robert Smith, CCETSW's Publications Manager, for completing the editing and production of this publication.

PART I

Understanding religion and ethnicity
in social work

Chapter 1: Introduction
by Naina Patel, Don Naik and Beth Humphries

This book is about the implications for social work practice of the beliefs and practices of minority faiths. In our modern multiracial society it aims to establish teaching about religion and ethnicity as an important part of social work education and training. It does not take a tour of minority faiths but recognises their importance in informing the values of antiracist and non-discriminatory social work education and practice. The three parts of this introduction discuss (1) the complex roles of religion in its historical context; (2) why social work practice is the poorer for not including religion; (3) applying CCETSW's values requirements to the preparation of social workers for practice so that they are equipped to build equal opportunities and an antiracist social work relevant to our contemporary multiracial and multi-faith society.

1. THE COMPLEX ROLES OF RELIGION

For many years religion has been thought by theorists such as Althusser (1969) and Anderson (1983) to be withering away. Yet at the end of the twentieth century religion seems to have achieved a new lease of life, and particular forms of religious movement (especially fundamentalism) have become a vital force for (and against) social change (Sahgal and Yuval Davis, 1992).

Haynes (1996, p.1) defines two distinct yet related meanings of "religion". It refers, first, in a material sense to religious establishments (institutions and officials) as well as to religio-political groups and movements whose *raisons d'etre* are defined by both religious and political concerns. It refers, secondly, in a spiritual sense, to models of social and individual behaviour that help believers to organise their everyday lives. In this sense religion explains the ultimate conditions of existence. It describes supernatural realities using language and practices which organise the world in terms of transcendence and what is deemed holy. However, the second of these definitions needs to be placed in the context of the first so that the impact of personal belief on the practice of social work, or indeed of any human activity, can be examined.

The contradictory roles of religion
Religion across the world has always had contradictory roles, having been used both to oppress people and to support liberation movements. A classic text on

these contradictions is *The Meek and the Militant* by Paul Siegel (1986). During decolonisation in India and Africa, the churches initially opposed, then were sceptical and finally supported the idea of independence. On the one hand, religion was used as an ideology in the attempt to gain hegemonic control of subject people. On the other, it was used as a vehicle for mobilising community organisation, often to help fend off that control. Christianity and Islam adopted both roles in sub-Saharan Africa (Haynes, 1996).

Haynes identifies the different attempts to politicise Christian communities in Africa and Latin America. In Latin America Christian communities were normally galvanised by radicalised priests. The liberation theologians of Latin America are known worldwide for their mobilization of poor people against political dictatorship (de Santa Ana, 1979). In Africa (except perhaps in South Africa), religious communities generally failed to develop as vehicles of popular power.

For Mbembe (1988), modern religions in Africa created political space in response to the totalitarian ambitions of dictators in some countries. This is not to say that religious groups are only notable for their political opposition. Their spiritual and community influence is just as important as their concern to change material circumstances. In addition religious movements have also contributed to cultural, regional, ethnic, political and economic tensions which existed before colonialism.

In countries of the North, Christianity has been deeply implicated in power structures for centuries, its bishops at times holding political office and involved in the oppression of the poor. At the same time Christians have been among social reformers, as for example in nineteenth century Britain, whose tradition is carried on through such projects as worker-priests in France (Edwards, 1961), Faith in the City in England (Church of England 1985), the Iona Community and the Gorbals Group in Scotland (Harvey, 1987), all radical movements which see the purpose of the church as standing beside and struggling alongside the poor. The stance taken by these groups has at different times brought them into conflict with the governments of the day.

The varying position of women within religious groups is another example of the complex impact of religions. Under colonialism, the prevalence of Victorian attitudes towards women meant that most African women had no access to education and its associated benefits. As Parpart (1988) says:

"for most African women... the colonial period was characterized by significant losses both in power and authority... Western gender stereotypes... assigned women to the domestic domain..." (p. 210)

Mazumdar (1995) describes the oppression of women under Hindu fundamentalism in the postcolonial era. In contrast, in Nigeria and Senegal (Callaway and Creevey, 1994) and Sudan (Bernal, 1994), religious-based women's organisations have mobilized to create new kinds of political roles for women. Women's Islamic groups are examples of popular religious organisations, especially in countries such as Nigeria and Senegal, where they serve to support women's liberation against male repression. Such groups have skilfully used Islamic precepts to their advantage.

In Britain those in favour of the admission of women to the priesthood in the Church of England have gained an uneasy victory. However, in the Roman Catholic church, the traditionalists still hold the upper hand.

So, as shown above, religious belief is a highly heterogeneous phenomenon which can be used as a weapon against subordinate groups, or can be mobilised in struggles against inequality.

Religion and the state

In a number of countries the state and religion are intimately intertwined. Saudi Arabia and Iran describe themselves as Islamic states, while in Ireland and the United States religious beliefs have influenced legislation and institutions of government.

In Britain, the Queen is the titular head of the Church of England and the Church of Scotland. The bishops are members of the House of Lords in the British Parliament. The Prime Minister appoints the Archbishop of Canterbury. It is not clear whether a non-Christian can become a British Prime Minister (Disraeli converted from Judaism), while a Roman Catholic certainly cannot be monarch. The blasphemy law protects the Church of England from attacks which are legal against other religions. The monarch is "Defender of the Faith" (though Prince Charles, in an acknowledgement of a multi-faith society, has declared that he will be defender of the *faiths*).

However, the link between religion and the State in Britain is not just a relic of

history. The Education Reform Act 1988 required all schools to have a daily act of worship. Sahgal and Yuval Davis (1992) argue that in these ways Christianity is given an affirmed legal status as the "ideological cement of national culture". This construction, they say, assumes a correspondence between national and religious identity, which means that members of non-Established churches, and especially non-Christians, can be only partial members of the British national collectivity. They are defined, to a greater or lesser extent, as outsiders. "Christianity, therefore, is one of the most important bases for inherent racism in the hegemonic notion of Englishness" (p. 13).

Recent immigration legislation vividly illustrates these points, affecting people's refugee status, policing employment, restricting welfare entitlement and allowing increased power of deportation (Cohen, 1996). This legislation has its greatest impact on black people, especially those from the Indian sub-continent, who are likely to be non-Christian.

Over the past 17 years in Britain the government has married social policy changes to a particular interpretation of the state religion:

> "Christianity is about spiritual redemption, not social reform... we are told that we must work and use our talents to create wealth. If a man will not work, he shall not eat, wrote St Paul to the Thessalonians. Indeed abundance rather than poverty has a legitimacy which derives from the very nature of creation... But it is not the creation of wealth that is wrong but love of money for its own sake. The spiritual dimension comes in deciding what to do with the wealth. How could we respond to the many calls for help, or invest in the future, or support the wonderful artists and craftsmen whose work also glorifies God, unless we had first worked hard and used our talents to create the necessary wealth... any set of social and economic arrangements which is not founded on the acceptance of individual responsibility will do nothing but harm..."

These are extracts from Margaret Thatcher's speech to the General Assembly of the Church of Scotland on 21 May 1988 (see Alison and Edwards (1990) for the whole speech). Thatcher ends her speech by unmistakably linking religion with nationalism: "I always think that the whole debate about the Church and the State has never yielded anything comparable in insight to that beautiful hymn, *I vow to thee my country*. It begins with a triumphant assertion of what might be described as secular patriotism, a noble thing indeed in a country like ours,

"I vow to thee my country, all earthly things above
Entire and whole and perfect the service of my love."

These sentiments have been used in the construction of an emotional and xenophobic national identity made especially clear in the Falklands conflict, in the Gulf war, in dealings with the European Community, in immigration policy, in health issues, in education and in ideologies which inform thinking about law and order and the welfare state (see the reports on the Conservative Party conference, *Observer* 15.10.95). In its varied ways, religion is alive and well and embedded in the institutional structures of contemporary Britain. This is not to suggest that Mrs Thatcher spoke on behalf of the Christian church, and many church members have opposed this incorporation of Christianity into a nationalist stance. Nevertheless the example serves to illustrate how privilege accorded any religion through legislation can be used to exclude those without the appropriate religious affiliation, from cultural ideas about "nationality".

Fundamentalism

The meaning of religious fundamentalism has become so confused by the abusive labelling of Muslims as "the Barbaric Other", that it has been suggested that the term should be dispensed with altogether. Sahgal and Yuval Davis (1992) show that fundamentalism cuts across religions and cultures and has often been incorporated into and has transformed nationalist movements. Such movements are basically political but have a religious imperative which seeks to harness the modern state and media powers to the service of their gospel. They have two features in common: one, they claim their version of religion to be the only true one, and feel threatened by pluralist/secular systems of thought; two, they use political means to impose their version of the truth on all members of their religion, and on others. They exist within all the main religions – Christianity, Hinduism, Islam, Judaism, Sikhism:

> "[Fundamentalism] can rely heavily on sacred religious texts, but it can also be more experimental and linked to specific charismatic leadership. Fundamentalism can align itself with different political trends in different countries and manifest itself in many forms. It can appear as a form of orthodoxy – a maintenance of 'traditional values' – or as a revivalist radical phenomenon, dismissing impure and corrupt forms of religion to 'return to original sources'" (p. 4).

There are examples of the rise of fundamentalism across the world, operating

both in state institutions and legislation, and in the lives of individuals. Some groups make claims to empowerment through fundamentalist beliefs and practices, and Sahgal and Yuval Davis (1992, p. 9) point to a paradox where women for example collude with and seek comfort within the spaces allocated to them by fundamentalist movements, while at the same time being detrimentally affected by them. Such claims construct constriction as choice (see Humphries, 1996) but within very narrow parameters, defined and implemented by those in power. As a general rule, fundamentalism equates with intolerance of difference and with extreme moral conservatism.

Religion and equal opportunities

Although it is seldom addressed, there exists a potential conflict between notions of equality and religious belief. History bears evidence to this in the subordination and persecution of groups by dominant religions on grounds of heresy, ethnicity, gender, sexuality, or disability. Each case was justified by reference to divine truth.

Modern forms of such persecution range from exclusions of particular groups to ethnic cleansing including systematic rape and murder as in parts of former Yugoslavia and Ruanda. Some religious-based social work agencies have expressed reservations about treating homosexuals as equal to heterosexuals, and at least one, the Church of England Children's Society, has stated that it will not consider gay men or lesbians as potential foster carers or adoptive parents (Pilkington, 1994).

Most people entering social work would not condone the killing of people simply on the grounds of their social identity. However, some see no contradiction between this stance and the social exclusion of groups on similar grounds. Students (and others) with religious convictions can accept equal opportunities, except for women, lesbians and gays, or whoever. This is not to say that *all* religious people hold this view, nor that *only* religious people hold it. The difference seems to be that the prejudice is justified by religious convictions and therefore takes on the aura of the sacred rather than the profane (as in blind prejudice which has no rationale). Some social work courses known to us have admitted students on the grounds that their religious beliefs are sincerely held and therefore excusable, especially if the students are from minority groups themselves.

This point has implications for the selection of students for social work

programmes. First, if programmes have adopted a policy of selecting candidates with values compatible with notions of equality, this principle is contravened if they admit people with fixed views about who or what behaviour is "normal", whatever their personal characteristics or experiences of oppression. Where programmes accept people largely or solely on grounds of "race", disability, or gender, etc. they store up problems later on in relations with peers or tutors, or on placement or written work.

The most thorny issue seems to relate to black students and religious beliefs about sexual orientation. It appears to be easier to reject a white candidate who is homophobic. There should be no confusion about this – there are enough black people (some of them with religious beliefs which are just as sincere) who can be admitted to social work courses, who meet the values criteria, without taking in people who are unsuitable for the work. Religious groups and people are not homogeneous in their beliefs. The Lesbian and Gay Christian Movement, for example, campaigns for their conviction that same-sex relationships are entirely compatible with Christian faith. A recent publication, *We Were Baptised Too* (Alexander and Preston, 1996) has a Foreword by Desmond Tutu, former Archbishop of Cape Town.

A second point concerns the way we think about equal opportunities. We do not intend to address the controversies about the meaning of equal opportunities, save to say that its meaning is contested (Jewson and Mason, 1992). Rather our point concerns the construction of equal opportunities policies as condemning a litany of discriminations against groups who are perceived to be disadvantaged. Some equal opportunities statements include religious beliefs, so ignoring contradictions between the content of these beliefs and other parts of the litany. Some religious beliefs legitimate the unequal status of women, or homosexuals, for example. This illustrates the problems of lists which are potentially endless and contradictory.

Lists also invoke dualistic thinking, a central ideological component of all systems of domination in Western society, leading to competition for scarce resources, and the creation of impossible choices such as whether to affiliate with, say, the black group or the women's group or the disability group. bell hooks (1987) advocates "the eradication of domination and elitism in all human relationships":

"... it is necessary to struggle to eradicate the ideology of domination that permeates Western culture on various levels as well as a commitment to

reorganizing society so that the self-development of people can take precedence over imperialism, economic expansion, and material desires" (p. 69).

This position draws attention to relations of power at interpersonal, institutional and international levels. It also acknowledges that groups who have suffered domination are themselves capable of oppressing others, that there is nothing in the *essence* of some groups which makes them incapable of dominating others – either inside or external to their communities. Moreover, it is a position which engages participants in struggle rather than a passive "non-discriminatory" stance. And as hooks says, struggle is rarely safe or pleasurable (p. 73). In particular, it demands that domination in whatever form be resisted, even where the lifestyle of those subordinated is personally distasteful.

Conclusion
Religion plays a complex role worldwide, at international, national, organisational, group and personal levels. A wide range of groups, sometimes with directly conflicting views, claim religious authority for their beliefs and practices. Human beings are able to commit unbelievable atrocities in the name of religion, and to rise to heights of courage and sacrifice for their faith. Any profession which aims to understand the underlying motivation of people should not ignore the place of religion in their lives, in all its contradictory – but very powerful – manifestations. To promote understanding of these complexity of roles which religion plays in the lives of users and professional social workers is the purpose of the next section.

2. THE PRACTICE OF SOCIAL WORK

Social work practice began in religious activities for charity and social justice. As social work has aspired to professional status grounded in scientific knowledge and method so it has distanced itself from religion. The profession's struggle to give its activities a solid rationale has in its wake de-emphasised religion and its relevance to social work practice.

Charlotte Towle (1965), an eminent social work educationist, underlines the importance of taking into account the spiritual needs of users so that fullness of the human dignity and potential is recognised and respected in all helping situations. Felix Biesteck (1957), Roman Catholic priest and another social work educationist, in enunciating the principles of social work also incorporated

religious thinking in its knowledge base and practice theory.

Contemporary recognition of religion

Interest in religious matters among social workers is beginning to surface on account of the Children Act 1989 and pressures from users who see their salvation in religion and whose morality and values are also bound up in religious beliefs. Religion is a basic aspect of human experience, both within and outside the context of religious institutions. Among some people, religion is an actual "way of life".

It is now recognised that the multiracial nature of our society has within it many multi-faith religions. The time has come for social work practitioners and educationists through research, theory building and practice to evaluate the role of religion and its impact for users and social work.

Religion in social work on the rare occasions it is discussed is generally focused on separate issues of religious or philosophical belief systems, without any reference to how one affects the other. Social work therefore needs to develop a common framework within which the spiritual needs of users of diverse faiths can be addressed. A core philosophical and religious knowledge base can then be taught.

Enabling users and social workers

Social work students and practitioners are left to formulate their own value base and moral code. Increasingly this individual philosophy, values and morality is leaving social workers short changed when practising within a multi-faith society. There is a clear absence of shared perspectives between social workers of diverse religious orientations. How can social workers help users to face suffering and alienation with courage, dignity and autonomy? How can their personal search for meaning be encouraged by caring and mutually fulfilling relationships?

The spiritual aspect of this search for meaning emphasises personal experience and action rather than doctrinaire adherence. Taking this position, the care relationship should encourage an open dialogue between the social worker and the user – an "I – Thou" relationship (Krill, 1978). This relationship helps the user overcome both social institutional oppression and psychological barriers to the expression of freedom and dignity.

The main aim of the care relationship is to enable the user to satisfy needs for

subsistence, nurturing and loving relationships as well as to discover meaning in life. A social worker in a care relationship that is sensitive to the spirituality of the user will demonstrate generic skills such as empathy, listening, acceptance and tolerance in all social work settings. Social workers' approaches to practice should go beyond remedial treatment of symptoms of suffering and alienation to address underlying social structural and existential processes.

Spirituality can be defined as the human search for personal meaning and mutually fulfilling relationships between people, between people and the natural environment, and between religious people and God, Allah, Rama, Christ or Buddha. This holistic view of spirituality has implications for these relationships and for relationships between users and professional helpers. In these terms, social work practice can be described as a spiritual voyage which involves promoting the growth and fulfilment of user, professional helper, and the wider community.

Including spirituality in social work education could influence the social worker's motivation and develop their helping styles, techniques, and selection of theoretical approaches. It can also attune the social worker to responding to users' implicit and explicit spiritual concerns. Religious language and techniques could be used by social workers at the user's request. Such practice may also be appropriate when a user holds the same beliefs as the social worker. The following example illustrates both these positions.

Case example
A Hindu user in contact with a social worker on account of his wife's illness, eventually had to seek help from an agency to have his child placed long term with a substitute family.

When the referral was first made to the agency, details of the child's birth and early life were recorded. During this process of this discussion the user talked about his child's birth being on the same (auspicious) day when Lord Krishna was born.

In the final stage of placing the child with a substitute family, the user was overcome with grief and loss of his child He also condemned himself for not being able to carry out his parental duty, and talked of his inability to look after his child as a violation of his dharma (religious duty).

The social worker, in the counselling process, recalled the user's previous statement that his child's birthday was on the same day as Krishna Jayanti (Lord Krishna's birthday). This led the user to look at the religious perspective of his situation. Using the story of Lord Krishna the social worker talked of Krishna's separation from his birth mother as she was unable to protect him. The user in understanding the idea of Yashodama looking after Krishna, saw his own situation less critically. He rationalised the substitute care provided for his son as an equivalent to Yashodama, caring for Krishna. This enabled him to learn to cope with the loss of his child.

The user-centred orientation of the social worker enabled her to apply care techniques based on religious teachings. Thus responding to the spiritual need and mode of expression of her user, with sensitivity and affirmation. The application of specific religious care techniques enabled the user to understand his predicament.

The nature of the professional care relationship

The user's preference and goal should be the primary concern of the social worker when applying their understanding of religion. The professional care relationship must be an expression of the social worker's spiritual commitment to compassion and social justice – an "I" who emphatically relates with a "Thou". In such a relationship the worker grows with the user, acknowledging the religious and professional influences on their practice.

When beliefs are not shared, the social worker should adopt a spiritually sensitive approach by attuning to the specific beliefs and needs of the user, without imposing their own religious beliefs. Insights and techniques from religious traditions other than one's own, such as meditation or consulting with religious leaders can be incorporated into social work practice, thereby widening its scope (Brandon, 1979).

This approach means that social workers of various faiths and spiritual orientations are capable of responding to the diverse spiritual needs and modes of expression of their users with sensitivity, while affirming the principle of user-self determination. The user's preferences and goals should always be the primary concern when applying specific religious helping techniques.

Social workers who do not share the spiritual orientation of their users may need to learn how to help users pursue their chosen religious interests. Likewise,

social workers who do not share their users regard for religious scriptures or writings may wish to give serious consideration to works that are important to the user. When the social worker feels uncomfortable in using a religious or spiritual practice desired by the user, referral to the appropriate clergy, immam, priest or monk should be made. The religious community support system of the user can also be used as a network and team approach to social work practice. Like so many areas of human relationships and belief systems, the social worker should not be surprised at the range of interpretations assigned to specific religious custom and thought. When added to the repertoire of other social work theories available they make the task of social work special and challenging. But in the last analysis professionals have to determine the solutions and make judgements. Nevertheless, Bishop David Jenkins (1997) may help here:

> "We live in a pluralistic culture – so whose religious values should be adhered to? Quite apart from the fact... the religion has yet to be formulated in which all the adherents agree about anything of importance, save that it is important." (p. 23)

Conclusion

This section has sought to foster dialogue between practitioners of different religious faiths and perspectives in order to develop a common framework. This framework could address the needs of users of diverse faiths living in today's multicultural Britain and indeed in wider European societies where religious practice of minority ethnic groups, as in Britain, have informed the development of social care provision. If today's social workers are to work within such frameworks, how should their education and training be viewed? This is explored in the next section with reference to CCETSW's value requirements.

3. THE PREPARATION OF SOCIAL WORKERS

Meeting realities

"Are you a Protestant?" began an article in *The Observer* (26 May 1996) by David Harrison on "bridging the sectarian divide". The question was put to an Anglican Bishop Michael Henshall in Liverpool. He said "the word Protestant gets overplayed... There used to be Protestants and Catholics in Liverpool. Now Anglicans in a city proud of its achievements in breaking down barriers between the two faiths over the past 20 years have almost banned the word Protestant, believing it smacks of sectarianism." Similarly, in housing and social service provision to for example, Asian older people, there are a growing number of

multi-faith schemes with Sikh, Muslim and Hindu elders making use of or managing day-centres/sheltered housing. Such individuals have age and ethnicity in common but come from different religious backgrounds. Unity in diversity is visibly and practically operated. That is not to say that every day, all is perfect and everyone has harmonious relationships. After all, today's Britons belong to a wide range of faiths, with complex philosophies, practices, politics and hopes. Inevitably with human relationships, religious and spiritual differences are often a source of strength as well as conflict as explained in the first part of this chapter.

In a document produced by the Islamic Academy and the Department of Education at Cambridge, Christian, Islamic, Jewish, Hindu, Buddhist and Sikh contributors (1991) jointly identified common beliefs and values in British society as being:
a "Belief in the existence of the spiritual dimension in each human being;
b "Belief in eternal and fundamental values, such as Truth, Justice, Righteousness, Mercy, Love, Compassion and care towards all creation. These values are to be found reflected in the human self and need to be encouraged, nurtured, refined and developed so that such seeds may grow, flourish and blossom;
c "Belief in a Transcendental Reality;
d "Belief in the need for Divine (or Transcendental) guidance."(p. 8).

CCETSW's values requirements
CCETSW's Rules and Requirements for the Diploma in Social Work (DipSW) makes explicit the purpose of social work which is:

> "... to enable children, adults, families, groups and communities to function, participate and develop in society. Social workers practise in a society of complexity, change and diversity, and the majority of people to whom they provide services, are among the most vulnerable and disadvantaged in that society."
> (CCETSW 1996, p. 16)

As to the values of social work, the requirements go on to state that:

> "Social workers practise in social settings characterised by enormous diversity. This diversity is reflected through religion, ethnicity, culture, language, social status, family structure and life style... They must be self aware and critically reflective, and their practice must be founded on, informed by and capable of being judged against a clear value base." (p.18)

To be successful in gaining an award of the DipSW, six value requirements have to be demonstrated in meeting the core competences (communicate and engage; promote and enable; assess and plan; intervene and provide services; work in organisations and develop professional competence). The value requirements are that students must:

- identify and question their own values and prejudices, and their implications for practice;
- respect and value uniqueness and diversity, and recognise and build on strengths;
- promote people's rights to choice, privacy, confidentiality and protection, while recognising and addressing the complexities of competing rights and demands;
- assist people to increase control of and improve the quality of their lives, while recognising that control of behaviour will be required at times in order to protect children and adults from harm;
- identify, analyse and take action to counter discrimination, racism, disadvantage, inequality and injustice, using strategies appropriate to role and context;
- practise in a manner that does not stigmatise or disadvantage either individuals, groups or communities (p. 18).

Social workers cannot practise these values and adequately support people without understanding what it is that they as professionals and their users believe. Religious and spiritual beliefs are critical in forming social and cultural values. Not surprising, therefore, are the references to "religion, race, language and culture" in recent legislation concerning children services, adult services and even criminal justice (Children Act 1989; NHS and Community Care Act 1990 and the Criminal Justice Act 1991 respectively). Government initiatives ranging from religion, race and health (supported by Baroness Cumberlege) to work with minority faith communities and HIV/AIDS (sponsored by the Department of Health in 1994) have followed as a result.

They also affirm the importance attached to multi-faith groups: "Faith groups have an ever more important role to play in counteracting stigma and prejudice offering in their place a powerful healing vision", said Baroness Cumberlege in introducing a report on HIV/AIDS/Sexual Health and Britain's Faith Communities (1994). Publications including those from the Race Equality Unit (London) have reflected this area, for example in the application of the Children Act 1989. What

is not available yet is a publication which aims to increase the understanding of the social work student, teacher and practitioner of values in the context of religion, "race", culture and identity so enabling them to discharge their ever-more complex roles in a diverse society as we approach the millennium. This publication is designed to fill that gap.

Extending horizons

Complexity is further added by the fact that several writers, notably Tariq Modood (1994), have highlighted the issue of religious identity in the context of racial equality. Modood argues that reliance upon "racial" categories has excluded the needs of religious communities like the Muslims. Worse still, he cites "same-race adoption and fostering policies which place black Muslims with black Christians, and Asian Muslims with Hindus and Sikhs; social work based on Asian needs which can lead to a Muslim being given a Hindu home-help who does not know about Muslim sensitivities or whose own inhibitions (about meat for example) prevent her from fulfilling her duties" (p. 14). Such examples in practice are legion. They demonstrate how restrictive are current interpretations of racism and the determinants of antiracist/equal opportunities practice which suggest that there is only one way of looking at racism. However, several writers in the field have for long argued that black and minority ethnic peoples' lives should be looked at in their full complexity. Just as their lives are structured by the daily experience engendered by "race" and class, so too are the range of belief systems and practices (including religion and its teachings) which sustain (and sometimes hinder) such individuals and their communities.

Black community and social workers will often provide a rich source of examples of how service users from the same backgrounds use their deep religious and spiritual knowledge to make sense of difficult social work matters and cope with them, drawing from their internal strength and support networks. Ironically this has been used to prevent appropriate mental health services being developed. Similarly black as indeed white professionals use religious and cultural knowledge to cope with intense pressures: one of us (Patel, 1995, p.34) writing on ethical conduct of "race" equality workers facing organisational racism said:

> "*She* regards racist incidents at work as so routine that *She* often disregards them. To be preoccupied at this level would mean that the changes and shifts necessary in employment, education and services would be sacrificed. To be surprised at their frequency would be to underestimate the complexity of racism. Instead the

philosophies of Her cultural background come into play: 'They say that the power of senses is great. But greater than the senses is the mind. Greater than the mind is Buddhi reason; and greater than reason is He [sic] – the Spirit in man and in all.'" (Gita: 3, 42: 60)

"Gita" is one of the most important religious and spiritual texts for Hindus. Hence the religious/spiritual dimension is very much a part of antiracist change and cannot be denied. In fact as Sivanandan (1982) has argued, religious and cultural practices of minorities are tainted with racist interpretations (witness the coverage of separate Muslim schools for example). So to think of minority religious communities without an antiracist perspective is to deny the overt and covert expressions of racism which interprets such religions and their practices. Such available knowledge together with recent publications (Modood *et al.* 1997; Inner Cities Religious Council 1996; Weller (ed.) University of Derby and the Inter Faith Network UK 1997) and others similarly available in the many communities, can only help to contribute to care staff's consideration of religious horizons in their practice and to inform the conceptual understanding of racism and its consequent antiracist practice.

Another example of religion reinforcing racial stereotypes comes from Scotland. According to Armstrong *et al.* (1989) "despite the fact that the Irish population in Scotland included both Protestants and Catholics, the terms 'Irish' and 'Catholic' came to have virtually the same meaning in the minds of many nineteenth century Scots. The Irish were considered by many to be a group of people whose historical origins, religious beliefs and class position confirmed that they were a separate and inferior 'race'." In this regard "racism was part of religious conflict" (pp. 26 and 27).

Such prejudices have continued into the late twentieth century. In recognition of intense anti-Muslim sentiment, the Runnymede Trust, in its submission to the UN Committee on the Elimination of Racial Discrimination, listed "ending of religious discrimination" as one of its recommendations with a consideration of "ethno-religious identity" based on the "concept of secular or cultural Muslim", for example. Enlarging this point at a European level, Mirza (1992) argued that:

"the large Islamic communities in the EC, the geographical proximity of the Islamic world, and the 'demonization' of Islam in the western media and political imagination raise the spectre of 'Europeaness' being defined in contradistinction to

'Islam.'.......the position of *all* minorities will be thrown into sharp relief by the European quest for identity as the majority cultures of the EC (and further afield) seek to integrate. Islam would perforce act as the *Other* for a variety of reasons. The focus on Islam was not intended to suggest that the consequences of ongoing events in Europe for other minorities were insignificant, but that Islam – being on the front line, as it were – could be treated as a metaphor for the serious predicament of all minorities in a changing Europe."

Not surprisingly in recognition of rising discrimination against racial and religious minorities in Europe, the European Commission has declared 1997 as the *European Year Against Racism, Xenophobia and Anti-Semitism* (COM/95, 134 OF 12 April 1995, para 6.5.1) with the Home Office having responsibility for organising the year in the UK.

REFERENCES

Alexander, M. B. and Preston, J. (1996) *We Were Baptised Too: Claiming God's Grace for Lesbians and Gays* London: WJKP

Alison, M. and Edwards, D. (eds.) (1990) 'A Speech by the Prime Minister, 21 May 1988' in *Christianity and Conservatism* London: Hodder and Stoughton, pp. 338-348

Althusser, L. (1969) *For Marx* Allen Lane

Anderson, B. (1983) *Imagined Communities* Verso

Armstrong, B. (ed.) (1989) *A people without prejudice? The experience of racism in Scotland* London: Runnymede Trust

Bernal, V. (1994) 'Gender, Culture and Capitalism' in *Comparative Studies in Society and History* Vol. 36, 1., pp. 36-67

Biesteck, F. J. (1957) *The Casework Relationship* Chicago University

Brandon, D. (1979) 'Zen Practice in Social Work' in Brandon, D. and Jordan, B. (eds.) *Creative Social Work* Oxford: Basil Blackwell

Callaway, B. and Creevey, L. (1994) *The Heritage of Islam: Women, Religion and Politics in West Africa* Bolder Colorado and London: Lynne Rienner Publishers

Church of England (1985) *Faith in the City: The Report on the Archbishop of Canterbury's Commission on Urban Priority Areas* London: Church House Publishing

Cohen, S. (1996) *Another Brick in the Wall: The 1966 Asylum and Immigration Bill* Greater Manchester Immigration Aid Unit

de Santa Ana, J. (1979) *Towards a Church of the Poor* Geneva: World Council of Churches

Edwards, D.E. (ed.) (1961) *Priests and Workers: An Anglo-French Discussion* London: SCM Press

Harvey, J. (1987) *Bridging the Gap: Has the Church Failed the Poor?* Edinburgh: Saint Andrew Press

Haynes, J. (1996) *Religion and Politics in Africa* Nairobi: East African Educational Publishers, London and New Jersey: Zed Books

hooks, B. (1987) 'Feminism: a movement to end sexist oppression' in Phillips, A. (ed.)

Feminism and Equality Oxford: Blackwell, pp. 62-76

Humphries, B. (1996) 'Contradictions in the Culture of Empowerment' in Humphries, B. (ed.) *Critical Perspectives on Empowerment* Birmingham: Venture Press, pp. 1-16

The Inner Cities Religious Council (1996) *Challenging Religious Discrimination* London: Department of the Environment

Jenkins, D. (1997) *Business ethics: A Christian Approach* in Marshall, E (ed.) *Working Paper No. 9705* the Management Centre, University of Bradford

Jewson, N. and Mason, D. (1992) 'The theory and practice of equal opportunities policies: liberal and radical approaches' in Braham, P. *et al.* (eds.) *Racism and Antiracism* London, California and New Delhi: Sage and Open University, pp. 218-234

Krill, D. (1978) *Existential Social Work* New York Free Press

Modood, T. (1994) *Racial Equality Colour, Culture and Justice* IPPR

Modood, T., Berthoud, R. *et al.* (1997) *Ethnic Minorities in Britain, Diversity and Disadvantage* London: Policy Studies Institute

Mbembe, A. (1988) *Afriques Indociles. Christianisme, Pouvoir et Etat en Societe Postcoloniale* Paris: Karthala

Mazumdar, S. (1995) 'Women on the March: Right-wing Mobilization in Contemporary India' in *Feminist Review* No. 49, Spring, pp. 28

Mirza, H. (1992) *Cultural identity, citizenship and social policy* conference at Bradford University

Parpart, J. (1988) 'Women and the State in Africa' in Rothchild, D. and Chazan, N. (eds.) *The Precarious Balance. State and Society in Africa* Westview, Boulder, Colorado pp. 208-230

Patel, N. (1995) 'In search of the holy grail' in Hugman, R. and Smith, D. (eds.) *Ethical issues in Social Work* London: Routledge

Pilkington, E. (1994) 'Anger at Gay Foster Ban' in *The Guardian* 28 October

Sahgal, G. and Yuval Davis, N. (1992) *Refusing Holy Orders: Women and Fundamentalism in Britain* London: Virago Press

Siegel, P. N. (1986) *The Meek and the Militant: religion and power across the world* London: Zed Books

Sivanandan, A. (1982) *A Different Hunger* London: Pluto Press

Towle, C. (1965) *Common Human Needs* Washington DC: National Association of Social Workers

Weller, P. (ed.) (1997) *Religions in the UK: A Multi-Faith Directory* University of Derby and the Inter Faith Network for the UK

Chapter 2: Ethnic minorities and religious affiliations: their size and impact on Britain and social work
by Kaushika Amin

This chapter brings to the attention of the social work world important concerns about religious affiliation and identity. Section 1 outlines recent statistics of ethnic minority communities. It looks at some of the problems of making estimates of ethnic minority communities and religious affiliation in the British context. Section 2 discusses religious minorities and diversity in Britain, describing the responses to the growing non-Christian presence in postwar Britain. Section 3 outlines some of the changing debates on ethnic and religious identities. Section 4 offers some tentative thoughts on the implications of these debates for the work of social workers particularly in relation to the Children Act 1989.

"The subject, previously experienced as having a unified and stable identity, is becoming fragmented; composed, not of a single, but several, sometimes contradictory or unresolved, identities." (Hall, 1992)

"Religious affiliation is at times a better predictor of behaviour (and perhaps attitude) than the group membership predicted on the basis of physical attributes or visible signs (phenotype). Given the significance of religion in cultural formation, friendship networks and identity, it should be regarded as incumbent upon those investigating the correlates of group membership in the field of racial and ethnic relations to include consideration of the dimension of religious affiliation." (Johnson, 1985)

"... If I am to make any sense of the Muslim in me, not only must I consider the problems of historical and cultural contexts and take account of the problematic relationship between language, knowledge and truth, but there is the inner world to consider... the decentred flux of experiences, and... the basic material we work upon in our journey towards knowledge of God." (Abdulla, 1992)

INTRODUCTION

The place of religious belief and practice is curiously lacking from most literature on ethnic minority communities. I say curiously because literature on ethnic minorities is very diverse, some emphasising racism, others ethnicity or culture. Religious affiliation is, however, rarely discussed except by those primarily concerned with religion and theology.

Religious beliefs are of particular importance to social workers and professionals who work with individuals and families, because people often turn to religion at times of crisis, during bereavement, family break up, divorce, etc. Many service users would readily identify themselves as Christians, Jews, Muslims and Hindus. Religion is still central to the work of most organisations in the voluntary sector.

I. STATISTICS

Population data
According to the 1991 census, 5.5 per cent of the population of the UK are of ethnic minority origin. The total population was just over 54.9 million of which the total ethnic minority population was just over 3 million. Nearly half of all ethnic minorities are of South Asian origin, representing 2.7 per cent of the total British population. Indians accounted for 1.5 per cent and people of Pakistani origin about 1 per cent. Afro-Caribbean people comprised the second largest minority group, representing 1.6 per cent (Owen, 1992).

Religious affiliation: some estimates
There are a range of problems connected with estimating numbers of adherents of different faith communities in Britain. There was no religion question in the 1991 census or earlier national censuses in England, Scotland and Wales except for a religious census in 1851 (Leech, 1989). Most sources therefore depend on data based on estimates, often from organisations within religious communities themselves. However, many organisations representing religions do not consider statistics to be of particular relevance and do not necessarily collect statistics effectively (Neilson, 1986). Organisations are reluctant to release membership information which may be used adversely by opponent groups (Neilson, 1986). Many estimates are extrapolated from the place of birth statistics from the 1981 census, the ethnic question in the 1991 census or limited surveys such as the Labour Force Survey (Runnymede, 1992). Some estimates are based on local studies and surveys.

However, there are no official statistics on religious affiliation or church membership (Runnymede, 1992). Government documents, for example Social *Trends* published by the Central Statistical Office, contain estimates which are likely to be treated as official. These are based on the data collected by the UK *Christian Handbook* which makes a distinction between "active membership", on the one hand, that is those involved in some kind of religious activity, and

"community membership" on the other (see Table 1).

Problems also arise from the distinction between "active membership" and "community membership". For example, "active membership" is different in different religions. In Christianity regular Sunday attendance at church is important in defining active. Differing practices relating to, for example, baptism – infants or adults – will affect the membership figures. Frequency of reception of Holy Communion may be an element in defining active membership in some churches. Thus the Church of England keeps statistics of Easter Communicants. But in most cases membership is based on Electoral Rolls. In Hinduism, prayers in the home are as significant as attendance at a place of worship. In Islam, attendance at the mosque is thought more a matter for men than for women.

The problems involved in defining "community membership" vary greatly from one religion to another. The social significance of Islam, and the sodal role of the mosque may be of great significance to the Bangladeshi population in East London. But, what does the label "Church of England" mean to a white East Ender who never attends church? (Less than one per cent of the population of the Stepney Episcopal Area are on the electoral rolls of the Church of England parishes). The debates about residual religion, folk religion and secularisation have tended to focus on Christianity rather than on non-Christian faiths which are newer to the British scene. Another problem in estimating "community

Table 1: Current estimates of religious observance and affiliation***

	Active Membership *(million)*	**Community Membership** *(million)*
Christians	7.23	38.2
Hindus	0.14	0.0
Jews	0.97	0.3
Muslims	0.51	1.2
Sikhs	0.35	0.5
Others combined	1.78	0.3

* The estimates in this table are drawn from the *UK Christian Handbook*

VISIONS OF REALITY

ERRATUM, 23 MARCH 1998.

Unfortunately there is an error in *Table 1: Current estimates of religious observance and affiliation* on the bottom part of page 22.

The figure for the estimated Community Membership of **Hindus** should read *0.3 million*.

membership" is of people who belong to a particular religion by virtue of their family background but are secular in their personal beliefs.

Finally, because much of this information is approximate, a great deal of disagreement remains. Figures for Muslim communities have been estimated variously as 700,000 and two million. Professor Ceri Peach (1990 and 1995) using a variety of sources suggested that in 1981 there were about 553,000 Muslims in Britain and by 1991 about one million, 80 per cent of whom are from the Indian sub-continent. Professor Muhammed Anwar (1993) using data from the 1991 census has suggested an estimate of 1.5 million as has the Inter Faith directory (see below).

Estimates for Sikhs have ranged between 300,000 and 500,000 (Owen Cole, 1991). Similarly, estimates of the Hindu community have ranged up to one million. A few years ago, Kim Knott, whose figures based on the census and labour force surveys have commanded much acceptance among religious communities, suggested that there are 357,400 Hindus and 269,600 Sikhs in Britain. More recently Paul Weller (1997) suggested that there may be around 400,000 Sikhs and 400,000 Hindus living in Britain (see Table 2).

Table 2: Estimates for the main faith communities

Bahai's	6,000
Buddhists	30,000 – 130,000
Christians	40,000,000
Hindus	400,000 – 550,000
Jains	25,000 – 30,000
Jews	300,000
Muslims	1,000,000 – 1,500,000
Sikhs	350,000 – 500,000
Zoroastrians	5,000 – 10,000

Source: Weller, P.(ed.) (1997) *Religions in the UK: a multi-faith directory*

There are also problems in examining patterns of adherence among Afro-Caribbean communities. In the Caribbean there are a variety of churches and sects. The writer Clifford Hill estimated that over 69 per cent of British West Indians in the 1970s before migration were members of one of the six main denominations – Anglican, Roman Catholic, Baptist, Methodist, Congregationalist and Presbyterian. If Pentecostal churches and other sects were added to this estimate, it would be reasonable to assume that over 90 per cent or most of the population were involved in churches (Howard, 1987).

It is also difficult to estimate the number of people of Afro-Caribbean origin who attend churches in Britain. Some suggest that around 20 per cent of the Afro-Caribbean population attend church (Howard, 1987). A survey on 15 October 1989 of 38,000 English churches including Church of England, Roman Catholic, Orthodox, Quakers, Seventh Day Adventists and others, suggested that 70,000 (or one-sixth) of those who attended church that day were of Afro-Caribbean origin (Central Statistical Office, 1993). The survey was carried out by MARC Europe and called English Church Census Day.

It is also estimated that a third of Afro-Caribbean church goers attend historic or "mainstream" churches, while the remaining two-thirds are thought to be involved in black-led churches, mainly Pentecostal and the Seventh Day Adventist Church (Howard, 1987).

The UK Christian Handbook for 1995/96 provides helpful estimates of Afro-Caribbean membership of different churches, although there are some suggestions that they may underestimate the figures for black Christians (see Table 3). At present the handbook does not offer data on Afro-Caribbean membership of mainstream churches. However, it provides a useful guide to membership of Afro-Caribbean churches. There are, however, fundamental limitations on any data on church membership. Often each denomination has its own definition of membership and this may vary considerably from another denomination. For example, Anglican and Roman Catholic churches often accept infant baptism as church membership. Baptists and some Independent churches require adult baptism by immersion as a condition of membership.

Table 3: Black majority churches*

	Members	Congregation
Church of God of Prophecy	4,938	86
New Testament Church of God	6,665	107
Pentecostal: Afro-Caribbean Churches	49,211	605
(of these some of the largest are):		
Foursquare Gospel	489	15
Church of Great Britain	1,000	10
New Covenant Church (Pentecostal)	3,500	20
Pentecostal: Oneness Apostolic Churches	15,069	212
(of these some of the largest are):		
United Pentecostal Church of Great Britain	2,900	17
Christ Apostolic Church Great Britain	2,000	4
Seventh Day Adventist	18,565	241
African Methodist Episcopal	300	8
Zion Church**	450	15
TOTAL	95,198	1266

* Most have at least some white members.
** Included here are some of the churches of African origin or some which have a largely African membership although the majority are Afro-Caribbean.
Source: Brierley, P and Wraight, H. (1995) *The UK Christian Handbook* 1996/1997 edition, Marc Europe

Absent from the handbook are figures for some of the smaller African churches. A useful source for these is James Ashdown's A *Guide to Ethnic Christianity in London*, published in 1993. He refers to the African Bretheren Connect which has a membership of around 10-15,000 mainly Nigerian and Ghanaian followers. Other

churches have East African, Ethiopian or South African followers.

There has been a dramatic increase in membership of the large Pentecostal churches (up from 44,000 members in 1985 to 49,211 in 1995) such as the New Testament Church of God, Church of God of Prophecy and of smaller, often local black-led churches. It is thought that since 1975 membership of Pentecostal and other Afro-Caribbean churches has increased by eight and four per cent respectively (CSO 1993, p. 153). This increase is a post-immigration phenomenon and many, perhaps most, members of these churches were formerly in the mainstream churches. The largest of the Pentecostal churches which has a mainly black membership, the New Testament Church of God, is based in Cleveland, Tennessee, and is a mainly white church in the United States particularly in conservative rural areas. On the other, its role among black communities in England derives from its strong presence under black leadership in Jamaica.

The Seventh Day Adventist Church is also based in the United States. In Britain it has been transformed from an ageing white, and often middle-class, church into a vibrant, mainly black church with a strong presence in the cities.

A survey by the Committee on Black Anglican Concerns, conducted in 1992 in which about 60 per cent of parishes responded, estimated that there are 27,000 black Anglicans, defined as African, Afro-Caribbean and Asian, in the Church of England. Corresponding with residential patterns almost half of black Anglicans (48 per cent) were in London, 29 per cent were in the urban areas of Birmingham, Chelmsford, Oxford, Manchester, Lichfield and St Albans. The remaining 23 per cent were spread through the remaining dioceses.

The survey found that black Anglicans were regular church goers, but many were not registered on the electoral roll. In parishes with a strong black Anglican presence, they made up to 4.5 per cent of the usual attendance, but only 3 per cent of the electoral roll. The result was that while 4.5 per cent of church wardens, who are elected by everyone in the parish, were black only 3.4 per cent of the Parochial Church Council members were black. There were 240 black members of Deanery Synods and 38 per cent of Diocesan Synods. Nationally 14 out of the 570 members of the General Synod were black; in the recently elected General Synod 13 of the 264 elected representatives were black or Asian (Gordon-Carter, 1995).

A 1985 survey of membership in Methodist churches (Watson, 1985) showed that

5.2 per cent of regular churchgoers were black. And like black Anglicans they were underrepresented in leadership roles.

Greg Smith (1992), of the Aston Community Involvement Unit based in Newham, estimates that overall there may have been as many 150,000 black members of various churches in England in the late 1980s. Moreover, the active black Christian community may total somewhere between 200,000 and 250,000 adults (and more if children are added). This would suggest that at the very least 10 per cent of the ethnic minority community are in some sense active Christians. Indeed, the figure would rise to around 30 per cent of the African and Caribbean community, as most of the Black Christians come from these communities. Nor do these figures include figures for Asian Christians for whom figures are hard to obtain but who are thought to number at least 1,500. Other Asians such as Filipinos and Chinese are also likely to include high numbers of active Christians.

So the black Christian community represents a substantial proportion of the total Christian community in England. In the past many joined black-led churches because they have been made to feel unwelcome in English churches. However, there is some evidence now that many black Christians are finding a home in mainstream churches and their presence is likely to grow.

2. RELIGIOUS MINORITIES AND DIVERSITY

One of the Oxford dictionary definitions of religion is "a particular system of faith and worship." This simple definition does not reflect the many difficulties inherent in any attempt at defining the boundaries of what is religion (Pye, 1972). One operational definition would be to say that religion is a system of belief and worship which provides its believers with a personal lifestyle and a world view. Alternatively religion is a system of beliefs and rituals linking communities to what they see as sacred or of ultimate value. Often it shows the way to God (or eternal bliss as Buddhists believe) and the way to conduct our lives. Religion offers spirituality and a code of ethics to believers.

In seventeenth century England an attempt was made to impose on the whole population "a particular system of faith and worship". The Act of Uniformity of 1662 attempted to bring the entire English population under one religious-political institution – the Church of England. "Anglican" became synonymous with "citizen". In fact, the majority of the population in the seventeenth and

eighteenth centuries, far from conforming to the 39 articles of the Anglican church, adhered to a system of supernatural beliefs and practices characterised by some as "popular paganism". In addition there were also Protestants and Roman Catholics who declared their non-conformity. The former included Baptists, Independents, Presbyterians and other Protestant groups.

The Act of Uniformity legalised the thinking that religious minorities were in effect non Anglicans (Ling, 1973). This conceptualisation still has resonance today. The growth of secularism among the non-worshipping majority and the growth of Methodism and other non conforming churches were part of the erosion of Anglicanism in the eighteenth century.

The Act of Tolerance (1689) saw an unprecedented period of religious diversity and tolerance. It granted freedom of worship to non conformist Protestants and although it did not apply to Catholics or Unitarians, worship by dissenters was tolerated. The Act was extended to Jews in 1846 so that the Jewish religion was recognised and places of worship and trusts were protected. As a result of the Act and other legislation, settlements of Jewish communities increased in the 1880s and 1890s and England was seen as "haven and protector of freedom" until the era of the Aliens Act 1905 (see for example Gartner, 1973). However, Christianity and the Church of England are assumed to be dominant in spite of evidence of the change in faith among ordinary people.

Theological research into different religious communities was well established before the second world war (Knott, 1991). Post-war literature by Geoffrey Parrinder (1994), Michael Pye (1972) and others brought to the public studies of comparative religion outlining in great detail beliefs and practice. Much of the earlier literature studied Islam, Hinduism, Buddhism, purely as religious systems but did not relate them to the British context, although these faith traditions were present, even on a small scale, in British towns and cities. There was little serious investigation into the content of religions and the factors of migration and settlement which change belief and practice in new environments (Knott, 1991). In addition, Islam, Hinduism and Sikhism were often mentioned without discussion about their internal diversification which continues to correspond to the patterns in religion from their countries of origin (Knott, p. 94).

The significant change in perception towards non-Christian religions in Britain was probably due to immigration and to their larger presence in some areas.

Before the 1960s, many Anglicans and other Christians tended to dismiss attempts at inter-faith co-operation as syncretist, a pejorative term suggesting a desire to mingle elements of different faiths together in a confused and perhaps dishonest way. This view still persists in some quarters. But inter-faith co-operation and occasional inter-faith services were growing throughout the 1960s (General Synod Board of Mission 1992). Many remember the establishment of inter-faith groups in cities such as Coventry and Wolverhampton in the early 1960s. Of particular importance to the development of inter-faith services was the presence of the Duke of Edinburgh at a multi-faith Ceremony of Religious Affirmation at St Mary-le-Bow in 1965 at the opening of the Commonwealth Arts Festival. In 1966, the Queen attended a similar service which has grown into the Observance for the Commonwealth Day which she now attends each year (General Synod Board of Mission, 1992).

However, the whole inter-faith dialogue was largely ignored by the mainstream churches in the West until the late 1960s (Cox, 1988). By the early 1970s, both the Catholic and Protestant establishments had begun to debate the relationship between Christian and non-Christian religions. The Vatican had established secretariats for dialogue with Jews, Protestants and non-Christian faiths. Similar moves were being made in the Protestant churches. In 1968 the British Council of Churches published a report which advocated "informed dialogue" and "sympathetic observation of the worship of other faiths" while ensuring that Christian witness is not distorted (General Synod Board of Mission, 1992).

In July 1972 the Methodist Church recommended that local churches should be in dialogue with representatives from other faiths and allowed the use of Methodist buildings for secular and social activities (British Council of Churches, 1972). A report published by the World Congress of Faiths in 1974 examined the reasons commonly advanced in favour of inter-faith worship and objections to dialogue. Thus by the late 1970s some Christian theologians had moved beyond a comparative approach to religions to an attitude which considered religious faith in traditional and popular practice. Evangelical and Pentecostal churches were and still are sometimes but not always opposed to inter-faith contact. Some of their members have refused to talk with BCC or WCF whom they saw as compromising the gospel.

This change in approach to religious diversity coincided with demographic changes among Asian and Afro-Caribbean communities. The reunion of families

of immigrant families throughout the late 1960s and 1970s also moved the locus of religious life back into the community. For example, in 1975, 18 new mosques were registered and in subsequent years registrations never fell below 17 and in some years reached as high as 30 (Neilson, 1987). By 1994 there were 380 registered mosques in Britain. In the early 1960s there were no Hindu temples in Britain; now there are at least 144. Afro-Caribbean membership of newer Christian churches also mirrored these demographic changes. By the early 1960s and 1970s the number of members joining black-led churches rapidly increased (Foster, 1992).

In the 1980s the awareness of multi-faith and inter-faith issues grew. The Committee for Relations with People of Other Faiths of the British Council of Churches published in 1981 *Relations with People of Other Faiths: guidelines for dialogue in Britain*, which outlined the theological and practical concerns relating to inter-faith issues. Other guidelines on the relevance of multi-faith worship and other related issues soon followed. The Inter-faith Network of the United Kingdom was established in 1987, providing a national framework for encouraging dialogue between different faith communities. Its membership of 38 includes groups from all faiths. By 1992 there were 38 local inter-faith groups active in the UK (Weller, 1992).

Some religious communities also feel there are legal inequalities between different communities in Britain. The Race Relations Act 1976 does not refer to religious discrimination, but is concerned only with discrimination on the grounds of colour, race, nationality, and national or ethnic origin. However, through case law it has been established that both Jews and Sikhs are ethnic or racial groups within the meaning of the Act, even though Judaism is clearly a multi-ethnic religion, and Sikhism receives converts from a range of ethnic backgrounds. Both have protection under the Race Relations Act and in consequence both are protected against incitement to racial hatred under the Public Order Act 1976. Yet Muslims do not have protection under the Race Relations Act or the Public Order Act, unless it can be shown that acts of discrimination against them are forms of indirect racial discrimination. In its 1991 Second Review of the Race Relations Act 1976, the CRE said:

"For many members of the ethnic minorities, their faith and their personal identity through their faith, and the reaction of the rest of society to that faith and to them as belonging to it are of the utmost importance. Indeed, for many, identity through faith will be more important from day to day than identity through national origins." (CRE, 1991)

In the early 1990s the CRE began a major new programme to seek support and advice on a private member's bill on incitement to religious hatred and to seek amendments to the Race Relations Act to clarify that an undue requirement on religious grounds may constitute indirect discrimination.

Many feel that the situation is compounded by the fact that British blasphemy legislation does not protect against attacks upon the religious beliefs of non-Christian faiths. Indeed, blasphemy law only protects the Christian religion, in its Anglican form as the established creed. For this reason, a case brought by the Muslim Action Front to prosecute Salman Rushdie and publishers, Viking Penguin, for blasphemy in his book *The Satanic Verses*, was lost in the High Court. This has contributed to the feelings of injustice and inequality between the status of different religions. Therese Murphy (1992), a barrister working on religion in pluralist societies commented that

> "religious tensions in Britain will continue to fester so long as the law on hate speech fails to facilitate progress towards a pluralistic society which is not only multi-racial and multi-ethnic, but also multi-faith."

3. ETHNIC AND RELIGIOUS IDENTITY: A CHANGING EMPHASIS

There is a vast amount of literature on the influence of ethnicity, culture and the experience of racism on the formation of ethnic identity in British society. Yet scarcely any has been written on the way religion may also affect that paradigm. Often religion is treated as a component of ethnicity or race (Johnson, 1985). In general religion is treated only as marginally significant in most studies of race and ethnicity (Knott, 1986; Henley, 1986). This tendency is increasingly being challenged by evidence suggesting that religious affiliation continues to be an important basis for individual and group identity.

Much of the early work on immigration and ethnic relations in Britain focused not only on settlement but also on religious and cultural practices. Studies such as *Dark Strangers* by Sheila Patterson (1965) focused on factors that eased assimilation and integration into the host community. Later studies, reflecting the racial ideology of the time, focused largely on ethnic and cultural differences. For example, *Between Two Cultures* edited by Watson (1977) was a collection of essays by anthropologists on ethnic minorities considering both ends of the migration process as a way of explaining issues in Britain. Religion was a key element in the background of ethnic minority groups. Much of the literature was descriptive and

focused on characteristics and needs of ethnic minority communities. Such studies also considered the way racial prejudice and discrimination may affect relations between white and immigrant communities.

The 1980s saw a promotion of ethnic identity based upon ethnicity, race and racism with much of the literature emphasising differences in cultural and social values. Commentators did provide useful information about the cultural and social differences between various ethnic groups but, some argue, they often neglected the experience of discrimination and racism in the daily lives of ethnic minorities in British society (Sivanandan, 1982). Meanwhile, religion as an explanatory category had disappeared during the 1980s from a broad range of ethnic and racial studies.

Writers like Tariq Modood (1992) started questioning the all-inclusiveness of terms such as "black" or "Asian" and argued that simple "racial-dualism" never adequately explained the experiences of minorities in Britain. What we have in Britain, he argues is "in fact an ethnic pluralism, not a black-white dualism" which does not dwarf class, employment, family, geography, religion, education and other factors.

More recently, both racism and prejudice against minority religions have become so closely identified with each other that to be British is often seen as to be white and Christian. In 1989, in the context of *The Satanic Verses*, the Home Secretary told British Muslims that they should embrace British ways and attempt to integrate. Some views seem to imply that it was not possible to be British and to be of the Islamic faith at the same time. In a speech in 1992, Winston Churchill, MP for Daveyhulme in Manchester, called for a halt to "the relentless flow" of immigration. He said: "The population of many of our northern cities is now well over 50 per cent immigrant and Muslims claim there are now two million of their co-religionists in Britain" (Churchill, 1992).

A report published by the Runnymede Trust's Commission on British Muslims and Islamophobia (1997) said that in the last 20 years there had been growing hostility and prejudice against Muslin communities. It used the word "Islamophobia" to describe this "dread and hatred of Islam and of Muslims. Such dread and dislike has existed in Western countries". The report draws eight key distinctions between closed and open views of Islam:
● whether Islam is seen as monolithic and static rather than as diverse, or as dynamic;
● whether Islam is seen as other and separate, or as similar and interdependent;

● whether Islam is seen as inferior, or as different but equal;
● whether Islam is seen as an aggressive enemy or as a co-operative partner;
● whether Muslims are seen as manipulative or sincere;
● whether "Muslim" criticisms of "the West" are rejected or debated;
● whether discriminatory behaviour against Muslims is defended or opposed;
● whether anti-Muslim discourse is seen as natural or as problematic.

Religious faith has an important impact upon identity not only through belief, rituals and practices but also in the way individuals perceive themselves in relation to society. Religious adherence often indicates individual and group boundaries between ethnic communities and society at large (Knott, 1986) shown by a small study carried out in 1983 by Hutnick (1985) which examined questions of identity with adolescents and explored the importance of religion. It was based on interviews with 105 young people from three ethnic groups, namely South Asian, Afro-Caribbean and English. The study found that nationality and religion "was an extremely important means of self-definition for the South Asian group". For Afro-Caribbean young people, "race or colour variables emerged as extremely significant" while their Christian identity was also very strong. Hutnick comments that the Muslim identity was underlined by 80 per cent of the individuals. Religion was slightly less significant for other young people, with 87 per cent of Sikh and 57 per cent of Hindu young people mentioning their religious background. Hutnick notes that nationality closely followed religious components and the "Asian" category was used only by 26 per cent of the sample.

Another study of 570 young Asians and 212 Asian parents, carried out by the CRE in 1984, challenged the popular stereotype that Asian young people participated in religious services merely to please their parents. The study described by Muhammad Anwar (1986) found that more than two-thirds of the groups disagreed strongly with the statement. It found few differences between the various religious groups. Both these studies indicate that religious background continues to be an important aspect of ethnic minority identity.

In addition, the importance of religious background and the strength of religious feeling raise doubts about the continuing use of the term "Asian" without further qualifications. Vaughan Robinson (1986) in his study of Blackburn illustrates the complexity of culture, languages, religious and ethnic backgrounds of people presently classified as Asian (Table 4).

Table 4: The composition of Blackburn's Asian minority in 1978

	Number	Percentage
Rural Indian Gujarati Muslims	505	29.7
Rural Pakistani Punjabi Muslims	361	21.2
Urban Indian Gujurati Muslims	149	8.2
Rural East African Gujurati Muslims	140	8.2
Urban East African Gujurati Muslims	95	5.6
Urban Pakistani Punjabi Muslims	94	5.5
East African Gujarati Hindus	74	4.3
Indian Urdu-speaking Muslims	47	2.8
Punjabi speakers from elsewhere	40	2.3
Indian Gujarati Hindus	40	2.3
Pakistani Urdu-speaking Muslims	23	1.9
East African Urdu-speaking Muslims	24	1.4
All Marathi speakers	23	1.4
Punjabi Sikh	23	1.4
All Bengalis	18	1.1
Other Hindus	15	0.5
Others	19	1.1
TOTAL	1702	99.8

Source: Vaughan Robinson (1986).

This breakdown provides an important picture of the regional, religious and linguistic diversity of Asian communities. Robinson comments that the "category 'Asian population' is in reality only a convenient mental construct used by the white population" which he says "rarely differentiate between a Punjabi Sikh or a Gujarati Hindu." In fact, "the 'Asian' population'", he says, "is a series of independent and different sub-communities" (p. 202). Race relations studies by the Policy Studies Institute in 1984 and 1993 showed significant differences in the economic, educational and social characteristics of Asian communities (Jones, 1993). Differences in voting behaviour, educational achievement, unemployment and employment patterns are indicated by other studies.

The importance of religion in self-description and identity was highlighted in the Policy Studies Institute's fourth national survey of ethnic minorities in Britain (Modood, T. *et al.*, 1997). The PSI asked people to identify key personal attributes "which would tell a new acquaintance something about me". The survey results (Table 5) highlighted the primacy of religion particularly among South Asian groups.

Table 5: Religion and colour in self-description

	Caribbean	Indian	African Asian	Pakistani	Bangladeshi	Chinese
These would tell a new acquaintance something important about me						
Religion	44	73	68	83	75	25
Skin colour	61	37	29	31	21	15
Weighted count	765	606	290	397	141	183
Unweighted count	580	595	361	538	289	101

Source: Modood, T. *et al.* (1997) *Ethnic Minorities in Britain* PSI

While scholarly literature has often noted the differences between Asian communities across religious and cultural lines, very little research has considered the influence of different cultural and religious traditions among

people of Afro-Caribbean origin. Beckerlegge (1992) says that this has produced a false dichotomy between a "strong" Asian culture and "weak" Afro-Caribbean culture. Religion, as discussed in the earlier section, is clearly important to a large part of the Afro-Caribbean community. The growth of the black Pentecostal churches in Britain has at least in part been associated with the experience of racial exclusion from mainstream churches, but also reflects a positive strategy for "identity fulfilment under conditions of struggle and social stress" (Pryce, 1979). Elaine Foster (1992) describes the structure of black-led churches as an inverted pyramid which are led by a small number of men but largely dominated numerically, socially and spiritually by women. For example in a moving passage about women's involvement, she says:

> "Women have created the context in which the social, spiritual and emotional needs of the congregation – and at times, the wider black community – are taken care of... The women cry with other mothers whose sons have been criminalised or involved in deviant activities. It is the mothers in the churches who, in the end, embrace the young unmarried mother and her child, even though the evidence of her 'sins' is there for all to see." (p. 54)

Elaine Foster, as do many others, argues that the churches have given black women and men self-worth, dignity and a positive identity, in contrast to the ways in which "white British society has alienated, devalued and effectively excluded them from the many forms of legitimate involvement in the wider society."

And other studies show that religious affiliation has an impact on the self-identity of young Afro-Caribbean people. Hutnick's study, mentioned above, found that while the "black" identity was being used by 39.4 per cent of his sample of Afro-Caribbean young people, it was equalled by reference to the Christian identity. The "coloured" and "black British" identity was used by less than 20 per cent of the young people (Hutnik, 1985). A study by Hiranthi Jayaweera (1993) of 20 women living in Oxford also found a very strong attachment to religious tradition among both young and older Afro-Caribbean women.

4. IMPLICATIONS FOR SOCIAL WORK PRACTICE

The influence of religious thinkers on the development of social work, alongside philanthropic and medical commentators is well documented (Parry and Parry, 1979). In part these historical roots explain the persistence of religious influence

in the voluntary sector and its demise in the statutory sector. Christian voluntary organisations, together with Jewish organisations, continue to provide a substantial range of social services to children, disabled people, elderly people, and other service users. Many of these provide counselling and other forms of support to individuals and families who experience problems. The ethos and employment criteria of most of these organisations reflect their religious roots although many Christian voluntary agencies are increasingly professional and secularised in their approach. At present, most ethnic minority voluntary groups are organised on ethnic and linguistic lines, mainly providing care of elderly or disabled people.

Social work literature on ethnic minorities has mirrored the changing emphasis on ethnicity and racism found in the discourse on race relations. During my literature search I found scant recent material on social work that considered in detail religion together with ethnicity. In general, most material mentioned religion in the make up of Asian communities or in examples cited of individual clients. Afro-Caribbean communities were largely described without any reference to religious and spiritual beliefs. It is this blindness to the importance of religious belief in belonging to a wider community which needs to be addressed urgently. For example, Ravinder Barn (1993) recounts her interview with a social worker who had placed two Asian children short-term in an African-Caribbean family:

"When asked whether a long-term Asian family would be sought in the future, she (the social worker) replied: 'Ideally, I suppose, it's difficult to know. I don't think we are particularly well off in terms of Asian foster parents. It depends which way you look at it. They (the children) are not particularly familiar with Asian culture. When asked what religion the children were, the social worker replied after a long pause by saying, 'I don't think I've ever known that'."

For over a decade, research about ethnic minorities and racism in social work has expanded. In particular, the need to employ black staff in all areas of social work, the need to develop ethnically appropriate services, and as highlighted by the case above, the contentious issue of "racial matching" in fostering and adoption have justifiably consumed considerable debate. It would be shortsighted to ignore many of the positive aspects of policy and practices from this decade that have developed often in face of considerable resistance from established institutions. However, the absence of a religious dimension needs to be rectified

if we are to avoid a social work that ignores the living complexity of ethnic minority experience. Sheila Macdonald (1991) in her guidance on the Children Act 1989 helpfully teases out the independent relationship between religion and culture:

> "In many families, religion is important in its own right, not as an element of culture. Here religious belief forms the foundation stone of family life and the culture which develops and grows outward from it; in this sense, religion and culture are an integral part of each other. These factors combine to make up an essential part of a person's identity and life experience and as such cannot be separated from her or his ethnicity." (p. 112)

What is clear is that religious identity is being asserted as strongly as ethnic identity in discussions about social care, particularly in fostering and adoption debates. For example, Sharah Sheriffi (1993) reported the case of a white Muslim boy placed with a non-Muslim African foster family. In this case, Muslims were considered to be a non-white ethnic group and the placement was therefore on the same-race principle. Questions have also been raised about the placement of Muslim African children with Afro-Caribbean families or strongly Christian Afro-Caribbean children placed with non-religious or secular black families. The religious background of foster and adoptive families is also of importance.

Aminah Husain Sumpton (1993) raises in more detail some of the issues ignored in the present approach to ethnicity and race. She describes the case of a 10-year-old Indian Muslim boy called Ali who was placed with an Indian Sikh foster family. The placement was a failure in spite of the same race background. The author highlights some of the issues. Ali was brought up to eat only halal meat. No pork product or meat was eaten by his family. The Sikh family did not eat halal meat, and ate pork but not beef because the cow is considered as sacred. There were differences in their names and in their clothing – the male members in foster family wore turbans. The foster family spoke Punjabi and English; while Ali spoke Urdu and English. So they were only able to converse in English.

All these cases highlight the matrix of ethnicity, religion, linguistic, cultural and other indices which form the background of British ethnic minority communities. For some children then, the impact of religion may be of such fundamental importance that other indices may need to be given a lower priority (BAAF, 1991). In other cases shared religion may be less important than ethnicity or even language. To quote an American author (Mura, 1992): "none of

these definitions stands alone: together they form an intricate, mazelike weave that's impossible to disentangle."

Religion is significant in a number areas of personal morality, for example, in sexuality, alcohol, drugs, diet, childrearing, discipline and education. Religious identity often transcends racial/ethnic background, especially in Christian and Muslim thought. Muslims often argue that there are no racial distinctions in Islam but one religious community. That is also the ideal for Christians (although in practice it is fragmented both by denomination and ethnicity). Some comment on the significance of being Catholic as opposed to Protestant (highly important for Irish or Polish people). In general in Christianity the more sectarian, evangelical or fundamentalist the belief, the more important the religious as opposed to the ethnic dimension. Thus a nominal Anglican is least likely to see religion as crucial to identity and lifestyle while a Pentecostal or Jehovah's Witness is most religiously driven. This applies across all ethnic groups. Awareness of this factor must have consequences in social work.

Without a more informed understanding of religious differences and ethnic influences, social workers will be unable to distinguish between the ways different individuals and communities may practise religious beliefs and official religious tradition. Often individuals and families practise religious belief more fervently as a way of maintaining links with the past (Knott, 1991). Community and family links are largely maintained along religious as well as ethnic and linguistic lines. Families with strong religious backgrounds often tend to conform to and identify themselves with certain traditional moral codes. Religious traditions are often patriarchal and oriented towards social control. And as we have seen with the black-led churches, ethnic minorities have often turned to religious faiths to reduce the suffering of living in a racist society. All these issues indicate the uneasy relationship between ethnic minorities and white communities and religions. They need to be considered in a broad range of contexts, from planning child care to work with elderly people.

REFERENCES

Abdulla, R. (1992) 'Where is the Muslim in me?' in *World Faiths Encounter* No. 3, November

Amin, K. (1995) 'Religion and Law' in *The Runnymede Bulletin*, November, No. 290

Anwar, M. (1986) 'Young Asians between two cultures' in Coombe, V. and Little, A (eds.) *Race & Social Work: a guide to training* Tavistock

Anwar, M. (1993) *Muslims in Britain: 1991 Census and other statistical sources* CISC Paper no. 9, Centre for the study of Islam and Christian-Muslim Relations

Ashdown, J. (1993) *A Guide to Ethnic Christianity in London* Zebra Project

Barley, L. (1987) 'Recurrent Christian Data' in Maunder, W.F. (ed.) *Reviews of United Kingdom Statistical Sources: Volume 20, Religion* Pergamon Press

Brierley, P. and Wraight, H. (1995) *The UK Christian Handbook 1996/1997* edition, Marc Europe

Barn, R. (1993) *Black Children in the Public Care System* Batsford

Beckerlegge, G. (1991) '"Strong" cultures and distinctive religions: the influence of imperialism upon British communities of South Asian origin' in *New Community* Volume 17, No. 2, January

British Agencies for Adoption and Fostering (1991) *Children and their Heritage: the importance of culture, race, religion and language in family placement* Children Act 1989, Practice Note 26

British Council of Churches (1972) *The Use of Church Properties for Community Activities in Multi-Racial Areas*

Central Statistical Office (1993) *Social Trends 23* HMSO

Gordon-Carter, G. (1995) 'Black Anglicans' in *Quadrant* Christian Research Association Newsletter, December

Churchill, W. (1992) *The Independent* 29 May

Cole, O. (1991) *Education Guardian* 30 April

Commission for Racial Equality (1991) *Second Review of the Race Relations Act 1976*

Cox, H. (1990) 'Seven Samurai and how they looked again: theology, social analysis, and religion popular in Latin America' in Ellis, M. H. and Maduro, O. (eds.) *Expanding the View: Gustavo Gutierrez and the future of liberation theology* Orbis Books

Foster, E. (1992) 'Women and the inverted pyramid of the black churches in Britain' in Sahgal, G. and Yuval-Davis, N. (eds.) *Refusing Holy Orders: women and fundamentalism in Britain* Virago

Gartner, L. P. (1973) *The Jewish Immigrant in England 1870-1914* Simon Publications

General Synod Board of Mission (1992) *Multi-faith Worship* Church Housing Publishing

George, J and Young, J. (1991) 'History of migration to the United Kingdom' in Squires, A. J. (ed.) *Multicultural Health Care and Rehabilitation of Older People* Edward Arnold

Hall, S. (1992) 'The Question of Cultural Identity' in Hall, S., Held, D. and McGrew, T. (eds) *Modernity and Its Futures* Polity Press

Henley, A. (1986) 'The Asian community in Britain' in Coombe, V. and Little, A. (eds) *Race and Social Work: a guide to training* Tavistock.

Howard, V. (1987) *A Report on Afro-Caribbean Christianity in Britain* Community Religions Project Research Paper

Hutnick, N. (1985) 'Aspects of identity in a multi-ethnic society' in *New Community* Volume 12, No. 2, Summer, pp. 298-309

Jayaweera, H. (1993) 'Racial differences and ethnic identity: the experiences of Afro-Caribbean women in a British city' in *New Community* Volume 19, No. 3, April

Johnson, M. R. D. (1985) '"Race", religion and ethnicity: religious observance in the West Midlands' in *Ethnic and Racial Studies* Volume 8, No. 3, July

Knott, K. (1986) *Religion and Identity, and the Study of Ethnic Minority Religions in Britain* Community Religions Research Paper

Knott, K. (1991) 'Bound to Change? the religions of South Asians in Britain' in Vertovec, S. (ed.) *Aspects of the South Asian Diaspora* Oxford University Press

Jones, T. (1993) *Britain's Ethnic Minorities* Policy Studies Institute

Leech, K. (1989) *A Question in Dispute: the debate about an 'ethnic' question in the census* Runnymede Trust

Macdonald, S. (1991) *All Equal Under the Act? – a practical guide to the Children Act 1989 for social workers* Race Equality Unit

Modood, T. (1992) *Not Easy Being British: colour, culture and citizenship* Runnymede Trust

Modood, T., Berthoud, R., Lakey, J., Nazroo, J., Smith, P., Virdee, S. and Beishon, S. (1997) *Ethnic Minorities in Britain: diversity and disadvantage* Policy Studies Institute

Mura, D. (1992) *Real Life Mother* Jones, Sept./Oct.

Murphy, T. (1992) 'Incitement to Hatred: lessons from Northern Ireland' in Coliver, S.(ed.) *Striking a Balance: hate speech, freedom of expression and non-discrimination* Article 19, International Centre Against Censorship

Nielsen, J. (1987) 'Muslims in Britain: searching for an identity?' in *New Community* Volume 13, No. 3, Spring

Nielsen, J. (1987) 'Other Religions' in *Reviews of United Kingdom Statistical Sources* Volume 20, Religion Pergamon Press

Parrinder, G. (1964) *The World's Living Religions* Pan

Parry, N. and Parry, J. (1979) 'Social work, professionalism and the state' in Parry, N. Rustin, M. and Satyamurti, C. (eds) *Social Work, Welfare and the State* Arnold

Patterson, S. (1965) *Dark Strangers: a study of West Indians in London* Harmondsworth

Peach, C. (1990) 'The Muslim population of Great Britain' in *Ethnic and Racial Studies* Volume 13, No. 3, July

Peach, C. and Glebe, G. (1995) 'Muslim minorities in Western Europe' in *Ethnic and Racial Studies*, Volume 18, No.1, January

Pryce, K. (1979) *Endless Pressure: a study of West Indian life-styles in Bristol* Penguin

Pye, M. (1972) *Comparative Religion: an introduction through source materials* David and Charles

Robinson, V. (1986) *Transients Settlers and Refugees: Asians in Britain* Clarendon Press

Runnymede Trust (1992) 'Data on religious observance' in *Runnymede Bulletin* No. 253, March

Runnymede Trust (1997) *Islamophobia: its features and dangers: a consultative paper*, Runnymede Commission on British Muslims and Islamophobia, The Runnymede Trust

Sheriffi, S. (1993) *The Muslim News* 19 February

Sivanandan, A. (1982) *A Different Hunger: writings on black resistance* Pluto Press

Smith, G. (1992) 'The extent of the black population in church and society' in Patel, R. with Hobbs, M. and Smith, G. *Equal Partners: theological training and racial justice* CCIB

Sumption, A. H. (1993) 'A difference of culture' in *Community Care* 17 June and *The Times* 11 June

Wahab, I. (1989) *Muslims in Britain – profile of a community* The Runnymede Trust

Watson, H. *et al.* (1985) *The Tree God Planted: black people in British Methodism* Methodist Church Division of Social Responsibility

Watson, J. (1977) *Between Two Cultures: migrants and minorities in Britain* Blackwell

Weller, P. (1993) *Interfaith diary of events and directory of interfaith groups and organisations for the* UK World Faiths Encounter, No. 3, November

Weller, P. (ed.) (1997) *Religions in the UK: A Multi-Faith Directory* University of Derby and the Inter Faith Network for the United Kingdom

Wilkinson, J. L. (1993) *Church in Black and White* Saint Andrew Press

Chapter 3: The case for religion in social work education: an independent view of social work and ethnicity

by Sunita Thakur

"People in this so-called caring profession are wary of terms such as love, kindness and compassion because of their religious connotations," says journalist Sunita Thakur. As an outsider, she contributes some useful insights to the debate on the place of religion in social work practice and poses some questions the answers to which are often taken for granted by people in the profession. She argues persuasively for giving sensitivity to religion an important place in the tasks of social work in the UK. The chapter is based on interviews with a range of academics, students, practitioners and managers in social work in the UK.

Social work in Britain emerged from the Christian ethic of serving God by helping those in need. Today missionary work around the world still continues and most societies practise social work founded on religious values in some form. In Britain, however, social work has become totally secular in concept. Increasingly shorn of religious overtones, two-year training and detailed guidelines concentrate on enhancing "professionalism" while excluding religion. This chapter is essentially a collection of ideas reflecting a variety of opinions and interviews on this subject. It is intended to provoke discussion and debate of the issue of religion in social work teaching.

Only a residual Christian value system is at work now in communities of both black and white social workers, says social work consultant Don Naik. More importance, for example, is attached to the individual over the community; the nuclear family over the extended; or indeed the rational over the mystical. By moving away from the didacticism of Christian ideology, social work professionals intended to distance practice from the missionary zeal of the past; to practise professionally, unfettered by moral dogma and in turn avoid the issue of the moral dogma of other religions.

Christianity has supposedly become confined to the privacy of one's home and heart; but have the other religions of Hinduism, Sikhism, Islam or black and minority Christian communities followed suit? The consensus view would be "no". Yet Jews, Hindus, Buddhists, Sikhs, Muslims and many others are here to stay; they are a part of the tapestry that makes up British culture. Often at odds with Christian culture in their ways of thinking and behaving, many people from non-Christian backgrounds interweave their religion into every aspect of daily life. Family occasions are often religious festivals cementing and celebrating

family ties. While there have been many changes and compromises made to adjust to the British way of life the old ways are respected and observed. Many would say that this cultural identity is the strength and secret of survival through the crisis and upheavals facing non-Christian families.

Some black clients in contact with social workers wondered whether the social worker was aware of how positive and nourishing were the many cultural contexts of service users in spite of the formality of some of the interactions, particularly between men and women in the family. One client commented that although she cared for him she never spoke to her husband about her problems, preferring to confide in her sister or even her daughters. Zarina Choudry of the Muslim helpline admits that some social workers cannot communicate easily with men and can end up unconsciously feeling hostile to the husbands and fathers they deal with. Yet at the same time concepts of oppression and the ideals of freedom and independence can be difficult to apply in practice as much for society as for the individual.

THE EFFECTS OF A PLURAL CULTURE

Underneath the surface of cultural diversity with its languages, shops, restaurants and festive days there is another reality; closer scrutiny reveals that by and large Britain is split. White and black communities inhabit different parts of the country as well as different parts of any city. Poverty undoubtedly afflicts a much larger section of the black community; caricatures and clichés are too many to mention. Aided by policies and institutions it seems each community is cocooned in a shell of prejudice born out of ignorance.

The community care legislation stipulates that there must be service appropriate to the religious needs of the client. Professor Chris Jones of the University of Liverpool argues that this is the start of recognition for the diversity of religions so that such barbaric practices as a Muslim being fed pork or a Hindu beef can be eliminated. Yet he argues that it is only pressure from the black communities which has forced these changes. Effective social work in a plural society must embrace plurality in a substantial sense, not merely by a few knee-jerk responses to some obvious necessities.

Don Naik argues that the client is the key; to be effective, social workers must recognise that ignoring faith can negate service users while incorporating it

affirms them. He cites the epileptic who believes he is being punished for some act in a past life. If the social worker can respond that while this may be true, the will of God manifested in this life is mightier than sins in past lives, the user will have been given help in words and concepts familiar and comforting to him.

To respond adequately, a social worker needs more than just an ability to recognise Diwali as a festival of lights, for example, or of Ramadan as lasting for 30 days. A keen understanding of the meaning of these festivals and empathy with the service user is needed. Empathy requires time, a precious commodity for the social worker, and understanding requires something more than just a basic knowledge.

IMPLICATIONS FOR TRAINING

The student must be given a knowledge base – a complex and flexible tool kit enabling them to ask questions appropriate to the circumstances. Increased awareness within British society of the practices of some religions has been reflected in the community care legislation, but Professor Jones argues that more than the obvious superficials must be imparted in the training of students. Knowledge of what Muslims eat or when a Hindu festival takes place certainly has value in training, but teaching at present is specific and limited and tends towards generalisation and caricature.

Teaching might include the Hindu idea of self-realisation or Buddhist belief in Nirvana. Essentially Eastern ideas such as that God lies within us and unfolds through evolution and self-effort are different from the Christian concept of an external, benevolent and forgiving God. Likewise, notions of sin are specific to Christianity. Some mention of spirituality as existing independently of any particular religion but incorporating the basics of many would be useful. One cancer patient talked of how it took his crisis to make him realise that, while he was against religion because of its dogma and prejudice, he was not against the idea of spirituality and having God as an internal and empowering force.

Highlighting the strength and importance of spirituality, Sabnam Dharamsy, of the Muslim helpline, says that as our lives get tougher and more pressured from external problems we need to make sense of things and look within ourselves when we cannot turn elsewhere. Indeed, yoga and meditation are increasingly seen as valuable alternative therapies. While training does not as yet incorporate them, social work trainers are arguing for more time to be devoted to a spiritual

component. Dr Beth Humphries, of Manchester Metropolitan University, argues that the anti-intellectual trend of the times demands that social work remains concrete and does not waste time on the metaphysics of theory. It equips students with a base of practical knowledge that is useful in the field, but many social work trainers complain that two-year programmes cannot instil adequate theoretical as well as practical understanding. An extra year with religion as one component of the extended programme is needed.

Students interviewed also expressed a wish for a more sophisticated understanding of the various cultures they will be dealing with. They commented that much of the information already imparted is useful but does not contain many actual ideas. Given the heavy workload, a religious component would have to be in addition to and not exclude other parts of the syllabus.

Black students often feel as resentful in the classroom as the social worker in the field. Too often tutors assume that because students are black they will understand the background from which they come. Even academics are unable to conceive that whole families may come from but choose to reject a cultural/religious framework. That option must be seen to exist, even in the Asian community. All too often, fearful of having to become experts, many begin to distance themselves from their cultural origins. "I'm a Muslim by birth but don't actually practise it" was a comment made by one social worker. In time this can actually help the climb up the professional ladder. The message is all too real: count as a black but be like us.

To be flexible one must have knowledge of the difference between a religion and its beliefs and practices and the routine cultural practice of daily life. The two are often confused yet many trainers are reluctant to bring out this distinction since it may make them appear to be too dogmatic.

This kind of knowledge would help to combat prejudice against people with religious inclinations which leads to "rationalists" being pitted against "spiritualists" and is so damaging to the social worker/user relationship. While other prejudices are scrutinised and discarded this one is invariably not tackled. As a result, the religious social worker may often be as inhibited as the religious service user. One social worker commented that, although he was religious and believed in Jesus Christ, he would never talk about it with users in case they thought he was trying to convert them. As well as providing religious expertise, social work programmes should face squarely these prejudices and inhibitions.

THE EVOLVING NATURE OF RELIGION

Many young people appear to be going back to the faith they were brought up with and then lost later in life. Their circumstances have encouraged them to re-interpret and re-define what they were taught so that they may make sense of their lives. Young Muslims can find themselves at odds with their parents and religious leaders whose beliefs they believe have become outdated. One Muslim journalist commented that in reaction to her parents' request for her to marry she studied the Qur'an more closely and found that, to be a good Muslim, one did not necessarily have to marry someone chosen by one's parents. The parents were following what they had been taught by the Imams; they were not deliberately misleading, only misguided. This view is shared by many Muslim women who, having been alienated, are now returning to Islam.

One sociology student claimed that the Imams' interpretations of the Qur'an are often so crude that they do not make any sense in young people's lives in Britain. Many such young people are not happy simply to believe. Armed with their education and rigorously trained rational minds, they ask many more questions of the religious leaders as well as going back to the Qur'an. All too often the Imams accepted as the highest source of knowledge are ill-educated and unable to understand the demands being made on the youth of today. Their teachings remain therefore rather formulaic and orthodox.

Dr Gamdhi, former director of the Central London Mosque (Islamic Cultural Centre), agrees that it is in the nature of all religions to evolve and grow. Without such changes, he says, Islam, like Christianity and Buddhism, would die out; it would stultify from within:

> "Faiths without such flexibility have died out in the past as others will in the future. The young Muslim is not doing anything new or wrong, this has always been the way for religions to evolve. Yet the main tenets provide an ageless framework within which the details evolve and reflect the times. Islam is as sensitive to change as any of the other religions. It is merely the prejudiced notions of the media that make it seem rigid and fundamentalist."

Michelle Masudi, an educationalist, argues that young British Muslims are looking to redefine themselves as "European" Muslims while their parents remain essentially connected to a sub-continental identity.

THE NEED FOR AWARENESS

Most social workers have little formal training in religion. Nor can they be expected to be aware of the subtle changes in minority religions. Over and above this inadequacy the social worker also has to deal with his or her own prejudices and reticence at tackling the user's beliefs. Social workers feel inhibited by the taboo surrounding this type of exchange, even if for the user it poses no problem. The user sensing the social worker's unease retreats into a shell of impersonal and secular language devoid of any true feeling or meaning. Depressed, lonely or already estranged, the user will be doubly alienated by this kind of experience. For some it is an insuperable difficulty which puts an end to the interaction, dooming the whole exercise to failure.

Just as a social worker should be one step ahead of what services are both available and fitting to the circumstances of the user, they surely should stay ahead in their knowledge of the cultural or religious context of the user.

RELIGIOUS VOLUNTARY AGENCIES

In today's diverse society, counselling needs are being met more and more by non-Christian voluntary agencies, which because of pressures on social services are taking many referrals from social workers. Zarina Choudry, a voluntary worker, says that the user should be referred to an organisation which understands their particular religious background. According to Sabnam Dharamsy, in cases of depression the user often knows what their problem is but needs to talk it over, which takes time and soul-searching usually only provided by a voluntary agency from the appropriate religion.

It has been suggested by critics from the voluntary arena that social work has become too fragmented because problems are broken down into manageable parts which are then dealt with separately. This breaking down may help tackle symptoms but does not get to the deeper causes including those which reside in the emotional self.

Most voluntary religious agencies have been set up on the premise that all human beings have a deep yearning for spiritual meaning. Alia Haeri, a holistic counsellor, believes that until you release a user's emotional pain, they will not be able to tackle the practical problems that their world creates. She claims true

empowerment comes from dealing with one's own inner estrangement and getting in touch with one's spiritual self. Although professional social workers also aim to empower, their role is very different. They spend little time counselling users, the remainder being spent on practicalities known as preventive and assessment work. The workers in voluntary religious agencies, armed with religious succour, conversely may spend more of their time counselling users.

RE-DEFINING SOCIAL WORK

Many social workers today would say that the bulk of what they do relates to administration rather than social work face to face with users. One social worker no longer deals with a whole family. Instead, a team of specialists is involved, one member dealing with the children, one with the parents and another with elderly people. This level of professionalisation fragments the social worker's effectiveness and makes the service less cohesive and effective. It looks at cases not as a whole but as a series of separate parts to be serviced when necessary.

To provide solace, human contact and counselling were once part of any social worker's raison d'etre. Not any more. Where assessment and prevention define a job that is cramped by stringent budgets, it seems unrealistic to expect anything more than the most superficial sense of religious knowledge from the social worker. More and more clients will have to be passed on to voluntary agencies, including religious ones, to tackle long-term ills.

The social worker supposedly deals with the "real" world as opposed to the ideal. While the diversities of religion and the hypocrisy of dogma once justified a secular stand, to exclude religion today is to be equally dogmatic. If the profession is to be re-awakened and social workers are to insist that they are first and foremost human beings relating to other human beings, then "knowing" your user becomes crucial. Many social workers are fearful of relating to users in religious terms because it might appear to be a form of proselytising. While the dangers of bigotry and hypocrisy should be recognised, it is perhaps even worse to omit religion entirely from training and practice. If social workers do not wish to reject the faith of their users in a move towards secularism – a form of proselytism in itself – a more sophisticated awareness of the user's spirituality is a must.

Has "professionalism" disguised the essential nature of social work? How can it have moved so far away from its original ideals without a murmur from those in

the field? Today people in this so-called caring profession are wary of terms such as love, kindness and compassion because of their religious connotations. To use that kind of vocabulary reminds us that beyond colour, class, race and gender differences, there exists a vast reservoir of emotions that are communicable without language.

One of the most common illnesses today is depression. One doctor commented that given the isolated lives that many people this can only be expected. Another social worker working with depressed Asian women commented that they were so low they did not even know that there was another way of being. Increasingly doctors are discovering links between emotional unhappiness and long-term conditions such as cancer. We do not know very much about religion and the healing potential of spiritual belief, but it should be given its place as another system for healing, like psychotherapy or medicine.

As the number of choices increase and the lines between right and wrong blur, the temptation to simplify our lives may be human nature. Yet a truly plural society must tolerate and actively embrace new ideas, not reject them. When in the face of dominant opinion, an unfamiliar idea is given room and respect we will have arrived at true diversity.

A SELECTED BIBLIOGRAPHY

I read the following texts to inform my understanding before conducting the interviews:

Brewer, C. and Laid, J. (1980) *Can Social Work Survive?* London: Temple and Smith
Halmos, P. (1978) *The Faith of the Counsellors* London: Constable
Hudson, B. L. (1982) *Social Work with Psychiatric Patients* Basingstoke: Macmillan Press
Northern Curriculum Development Project (1991) *Setting the Context for Change* No.1 in Antiracist Social Work Education series, CCETSW, Leeds

I am also extremely grateful to the many social workers, students, teachers, managers and service users whose views contributed to this chapter.

LEARNING RESOURCES CENTRE
Havering College
of Further and Higher Education

PART 2

Case studies of religion and ethnicity in social work practice

Chapter 4: The AWWAZ group

(NB: The author of this chapter wishes to remain anonymous so the name of the group is fictitious, bearing no resemblance to any existing group. Awwaz is a Urdu/Hindi word meaning "voice".)

This is a vivid account of the experiences of a group of mainly Asian women, of black Muslim, Hindu, Sikh and Christian origin, together with a few women of the white community, in grappling with the largely unchanging forces of human prejudice, power and behaviour. Why the group was formed, the local background to its formation, its formal establishment and objectives and issues faced are discussed in this chapter. The group found that religious morality has been maintained and used as a tool for imposing value judgements. Issues of gender, race, class, religion and identity in Britain are raised. Since this account was written the group has been disbanded owing to lack of financial support.

1. WHY THE GROUP WAS FORMED

The women united four years ago to form a group which focused on issues of gender, race, class, religious misinterpretation and identity in Britain. The families of these Asian women were first generation migrants from India, Pakistan, and East Africa who had experienced upheaval, migration and resettlement in its varied manifestations, whether rooted in economic pressure or in religious and political oppression. This background differentiated the Asian from the white women's experiences.

Our white sisters in the dominant white male, colonialist culture of Britain are confronting their experience of sexism within the western framework of feminism. We multi-faithed black women experience not only the racism of the dominant white culture, which either denies our identity as human beings or offers integration by way of assimilation, but also the dual denigration of our gender by males both black and white. If to be black is to be oppressed then the oppressors must also include black men.

The struggle of the AWWAZ Group is against a system which does not respond to women's needs across communities and countries. However, our aim is not necessarily to reconstruct ourselves on the white feminist model nor to deny its existence. We believe that we can confront our oppressors who are largely men (both black and white) without denying our identity which is both black and female. More importantly, we can do it as individuals with human needs of our own without denying the equal existence and gender of men as seen from our eastern perspective of being mothers, daughters, sisters and wives. For us to

adopt the white feminist model would simply replicate the exclusivity of yet another "ism" in society and would not provide a solution complementing our eastern identity and culture, much of which is positive and valuable.

Although we are from different religious backgrounds, our beliefs do not lead us to discriminate against each other or other members of the human race. We believe that our faiths contain the principles of equal opportunities and justice. As women we are able to accept each other as diverse individuals with varied backgrounds, experiences, and beliefs.

Our experience is that the use of religious morality to make value judgements about the rest of the population leads to division, exclusivity, and discrimination. All human beings, in our view, are worthy of respect and equal treatment, regardless of differences.

Sadly, our experience is that religious moral codes are abused in both professional and lay arenas. Consequently individuals are not treated with equality and respect. Reality falls far short of the ideal of equality for all, especially in terms of access to local authority, social, education and health services and opportunities.

Our experience is that both black and white male prejudice deprives sections of the population of equal access to rights and services. Although what follows is highly critical of male behaviour in our locality, this is not an attempt to pathologise either black or white men or their humanity. We acknowledge the validity and equality of the male gender while condemning moralistic misuse of religious and non-religious beliefs by certain groups and individuals, which would deny others their right to be treated with equality and respect.

2. THE LOCAL BACKGROUND TO FORMATION OF THE GROUP

The group is based in a region of Britain in which the Asian communities make up over 20 per cent of the white population. Unemployment is three times higher in the Asian community than in the white community. Where Asians are employed, they tend to be in low paid manual jobs. Less than one per cent of minority ethnic groups are in high level managerial posts in spite of being established in the area for over 40 years. A recent local authority report indicates that less than 10 per cent of available Asian women in the area are in some form

of employment. As the Muslim communities from different parts of Pakistan, India and East Africa constitute a disproportionately large section of minority migrant religious groups in the area, this case study will thus focus primarily on the Islamic faith with its localised interpretation.

All the main religions of the world teach their followers a type of positive morality. Islam embraces all manner of peoples regardless of race, class and gender, accepting them as equal before Allah/God – the same God as that of Christians and Jews. Islam advocates justice and equality for all peoples and both genders. It is not the Islamic religion which is at fault, but the misinformed male-orientated interpretation of it which socially and economically benefits men and disadvantages women. Religious ethics are contaminated by a male political and economic agenda, which turns women into dependants and, as a result, denies them equality, respect and control of their lives and the opportunity to contribute meaningfully to society.

The communities

The minority ethnic communities have been establishing themselves in this area for over 40 years. A majority of the people are Muslim, consisting of both Pakistani and Indian peoples from rural backgrounds. The remaining are Hindus and Sikhs.

The Muslim community tends to live within its own walls as a protection against internal insecurities. In contrast, the small minority of Hindus and Sikhs, being less established in communities and therefore more personally independent, tend also to be shopkeepers and business people. Individuals from all three communities traditionally choose to live together in extended families, if not next door as a secondary option then in the next street as a third. This preferred lifestyle has proved efficient in avoiding racism, in promoting tradition and religious practice, and in maintaining identity and control.

The area suffers from the highest unemployment and crime ratio and some of Britain's worst housing, which was the only type of accommodation available to first generation migrants. Single men had originally arrived from India and Pakistan via the selection process which allowed the youngest and fittest males to earn a living in industry, transport and refuse services. This work consisted of 60-hour shift work in the early days in order to support families back home and eventually to establish them here. There are reports that the Asian men were most often selected for night shift work in the factories and mills, which their

white counterparts avoided, and were not paid equal wages for this work. Lack of English language skills and impoverished formal education opportunities in the countries of origin have prevented many Asians from gaining access to services, employment, education, and information. This has exacerbated prejudice as the host community neither understands this alien culture nor its language. These disadvantages are doubled in the case of women who are dependent on their menfolk, and suffer not only racism but also the dual-edged sexism of white and black males. Experience of racism has led to a reinforcement of cultural and pseudo-religious values in an attempt to create a sense of stability and belonging in a hostile and alien environment.

Originally women were instructed to remain indoors by their menfolk for their own safety. This practice has developed into a defence of Asian male insecurity against the inevitable challenge of women seeking independence and being attracted by the alternative culture of the outside world.

The community participates actively in religious observance and has successfully helped to build large numbers of mosques locally, regionally and abroad. The Sikh and Hindu minorities still regularly travel eight to 10 miles out of the area to Gurdwaras and Mandirs to worship. Men and women from these two faiths are equally active in their participation outside the home. Indeed, facilities are purpose built to permit both genders to participate in religious and community affairs.

Muslim women, however, are not permitted to participate in religious or community affairs outside the home in this area, this being largely due to local interpretation of women's roles within Islam. The situation remains unchallenged, as interpretation by Asian males remains biased by the variables of gender, race, class and identity, resulting in religious bigotry and sexism which is adhered to regardless of one's professional status. Some Asian men, as is the case with some white men, are unable to stand outside their personal sexism and acknowledge the rights of women to the very services they are delivering. This situation prevails in spite of contemporary requirements to adhere to equal opportunities policies and practice.

Religious misinterpretation and its effects on women
The Qur'an has for many years been taught by rote in Arabic without translation or explanation. This practice parallels the reading of the Latin text of the Bible by Roman Catholic priests in Britain not so long ago. Indeed, services were

traditionally held in Latin and the words understood by few, particularly women who had little power within the church. While many Muslim children here are tri-lingual and only have the ability to read the Qur'an phonetically, both their linguistic needs and abilities remain unrealised, and more importantly their understanding of religious issues remains severely compromised. The Sikh communities, in contrast, have liaised with local schools and colleges to facilitate their children learning Punjabi for religious reasons in a structured manner with appropriate levels of accreditation.

The concept of Izzat

Within Islam education is largely considered suitable for boys, while on the whole girls and women from the Muslim community are actively discouraged from participating beyond school years. The picture is improving but at a very slow rate. This is due to the fact that marriage is uppermost in the minds of parents whose urge to do their duty becomes paramount at the moment of their children's puberty. The concept of Izzat, shared equally by Hindus, Muslims and Sikhs, describes the sexual honour and morality of a woman as defined within the boundary of the honour of her father, her grandfather, and the wider male community. Although the concept of Izzat within the religious context pertains to both male and female morality, pseudo-religious interpretation holds woman responsible as the sexual vessel wherein Izzat can be violated. It is parallel to the western concept of a woman's honour and virginity. It follows that if this female honour, Izzat, or virginity is defiled at the hands of the woman to whom it belongs, then so too is the very honour of the patriarchs.

Obviously it would take a man to defile female honour in heterosexual terms, as the alternative sexuality, lesbianism, is not yet a concept in the eyes of the learned patriarchs. Yet alternative sexuality for men has what the patriarchs consider to be effeminate qualities, and is given the concession of belonging to the Hijra community. The literal translation here means coward, a derogatory word. The question then arises as to whether women should seek parity with homosexual men when they are assigned to a lower category.

Thus the word Izzat describing a woman's sexual honour has become synonymous with the male individual, family honour and status. This scenario means that men have established themselves as the keepers or plunderers of female honour. Sexual honour in this case refers to a woman's entire sexuality including body language, clothes, hair and verbal communication, as well as virginity.

The entire life cycle and sexuality of woman must be strictly governed and regulated by her paternal relatives and keepers, as therein lies the potential to destroy the structure of male supremacy in society. Marriage at puberty is preferable in the eyes of most Asian parents from all religious groups to permitting opportunities for sexual experiment with its inevitable consequences at this age. Traditional interpretation of parental religious duty is justified and emphasised in the face of the western model of sexual experimentation before marriage which leads to one-parent families, abortion, and the looming threat of HIV and AIDS. Traditionally pregnancy outside marriage and abortion are considered to be major sins against religion, as in the Christian faith practised by a declining number of the white host community here.

Although greater tolerance and forgiveness are developing in the Christian context, most traditional Hindu, Sikh, and Muslim parents would be mortified at the dishonour of a pregnancy before marriage. Their interpretation would be that their honour or Izzat is forever lost in the eyes and by the standards of the communities within which they live. Death in fact would be preferable to the shame invited by their erring daughter – the western way is negative, Godless and without models, to be avoided at all costs, more so since the threat of HIV and AIDS.

As menfolk are not susceptible to pregnancy, nor subsequently easily found guilty of misdemeanour or paternity outside marriage, their freedom of movement and expression does not need to be circumscribed. However, parents are attempting to exert the pressure of their own experience largely in an attempt to secure the best available option for their children. It must be recognised that some parents fail to appreciate that the perspective of their offspring is now culturally and generationally different from their own and that traditional practices are not always observed with pure altruism in mind.

Interpretation of religious values from a patriarchal perspective and its effect upon women – reasons for the need for a support group

Women in our area are excluded from entering mosques (unlike in London and other Islamic countries) and enjoy no cultural or religious involvement outside the home. Here Muslim women are forbidden to attend burials and graveyards as the male interpretation of religion denies them this opportunity. The local cultural interpretation is that women are potentially unclean due to their menstruation and their presence would risk rendering mosques unclean, an irreverent act. The same fear of unclean contamination by menstruating women

surrounds the burial of a corpse, although this is ingeniously couched in concern for the weaker sex and the need to spare women experiences which would overwhelm them. This practice, however, is not indicative of all Islamic communities around the world where women do indeed participate fully in the burial of their dead. In other words here, in this locality, it takes a man to stomach such sights as death. In this way many women have been denied the right actively to participate in their personal grieving. Although many women do not have stereotypical responses to grieving, some report being psychologically and emotionally affected if not permitted to grieve naturally. Not all women wish to attend the grave side at burials of loved ones, but others do; local traditional practice takes away the right to choose. These are some of the implications of *interpretation* of particular religious practices rather than comments on the religious practice *per se*.

Hindu, Sikh and Muslim women are also excused from participating in fasting during menstruation as during this time they are considered to be unclean with the potential to contaminate religious books and artefacts. Women and men are obliged to perform ritual ablutions before carrying out religious tasks as a step towards preparing also for religious cleanliness. Ritual ablutions are carried out following menstruation, sexual intercourse and childbirth before women can resume their normal activities. The positive original philosophy of hygiene has become secondary to the pathologising of women. A live example of this is still practised in orthodox Hindu households where a menstruating woman must refrain from cooking, touching clean clothes, or movements which would contaminate the rest of the household. Ritual bathing and prayer would once more cleanse following the flow of the menstrual cycle.

A Christian woman used to be expected to undergo a blessing known as Churching following childbirth, to ritually cleanse her and prevent her contaminating the community. Muslim women are expected to follow a similar procedure. They are considered to be unclean for 40 days following childbirth and in orthodox households are expected not to leave the home until ritual bathing and prayers are carried out. The original concept allows for a period of rest and closeness to the baby after the birth. We women feel that this original positive concept has been pathologised. It seems that men forget who gave them birth, and the unclean route through which they all passed to reach this world.

Women in Islam have rights of ownership of land, inheritance and business, which should lead to a great deal of financial independence. But women in this

locality have been discouraged and prevented from taking active part in employment. The Qur'an is invoked by local males as forbidding women from carrying out work except in the home. Women who transgress this pseudo-religious dictate are considered to be of loose character as they have dared to disobey religion. They are treated as women who have no Izzat, or as women who deserve the sexual attention they attract by being out of doors. A woman's life therefore is to be defined within the four walls of her home. Dialogue between men and women is unknown. Such men have grown up in an environment of gender bias and so have limited tolerance and acceptance of equal participation by women, including white women.

Some beliefs about menstruation in traditional societies are surrounded by myths formed from a culturally developed interpretation of religion which serves to disadvantage women who seek to develop, change and exercise free will. More particularly, women do not have the tools of economic independence or equality to gain access to the education required to challenge these beliefs. Men around the world and their interpretation of religion, half-based on the fear of loss of personal and collective male power and half on culturally-based superstitious ignorance, determine the fate of women, remaining largely unchallenged. Our difficulty lies in enlightening the male and female traditionalists who hold the power and interpret religion.

Traditional male misinterpretation of religious morality and its effect upon women

Our entire identity is dictated within the heterosexual relationship and in the shadow of the male identity. We are only just beginning to dare to explore our pre-regulated and predetermined responses to sexuality. The interpretation of woman's role derives from Adam and Eve. Any challenge to this view has only recently been tolerated and reluctantly at that. We Asian women are conditioned to believe that we must only leave our father's house in a bridal outfit, and our husband's house in a coffin. Women are reminded of this in Indian and Pakistani films which show that the patriarchal family honour must be safeguarded above all else, including personal desire or other difficulties. Asserting personal independence is a sin against religion and a challenge to patriarchal values. Cultural practice operates under the misguided notion that Hinduism, Sikhism, Islam and Christianity authorise the male gender to dictate to females how to live their lives. Thus men are self-styled defenders of the faith where women are concerned. The use of brute force and mutilation are quite justifiable in the eyes

of those males who do not believe in persuasion, or have tried and failed to subordinate women. We ask as women from whom are we being protected?

While all of these major faiths expect the genders to show mutual respect and accept they are equal but different, males may be called upon to offer moral support and sexual restraint where appropriate. Women according to religious texts are equal in the eyes of their maker, simply as a different gender. It is this philosophy and truth which are at the heart of our group. Our situation in Britain today is outdated; it mirrors almost precisely the archaic position of women in the Middle Ages, under the supremacy and control of the male dominated church and its pseudo-religious practices in relation to women.

It is from within this social context that AWWAZ emerged. It must be mentioned here that the menfolk in our immediate families – fathers, brothers, husbands and sons – have largely supported our initiatives and upon occasion have acted as human shields in our extreme experiences of bigotry and sexism.

3. FORMATION AND OBJECTIVES OF THE GROUP

Before the group was officially established and made its first approach to social services for starter funding, many of the women were known to each other. We worked from home bases as having an external office was considered too vulnerable. The women included volunteer workers or workers with Asian women at grass roots levels in the fields of health and local authority services. These isolated posts were labelled ethnic minority posts but had no integrated management structure to meet their professional, training and personnel needs. These aspects of support were denied, viewed as peripheral, and the posts were usually on short-term section 11 contracts. However, there has been an informal mutual support network across departments and employers.

Over a number of years female support in the community was won through the maternity unit, schools, and clinics. Confidentiality has been the golden rule and a large number of women have been assisted. Women pooled their resources to raise funds for specialist equipment which would help women and children in the area. The experience proved that women from several different religious backgrounds, cultures and colours could work together successfully. The emergence of such powerful cross-cultural support was for us the official beginning of a group, together with a small grant from social services. Upon

becoming an official voluntary sector group, recognised by social services, we marked our launch with a publicity campaign and celebrations. At this time we naively assumed that our right to promote activities for women would be accepted. Sadly, we were wrong. We eventually had no choice but to revert from more open to more covert means of communication due to the hostile reactions we received.

Three main needs were emerging in our early days:

i **a support network for Asian women in white establishments** and within the non-western communities, which would recognise that we were the targets of not only white racism but also white sexism. Highlighting this need was an incident involving an interpreter in a maternity unit. It is not unusual for some women to give birth in the absence of husbands or immediate family, nor is any woman able to ensure she will give birth during the office hours to which the interpreters are restricted. Although interpreting services were meant to support patients, it seems that priority is given to the requirements of daytime bureaucracy rather than patient need. It is not acknowledged that the needs of the non-English speaking patient continue after 5 p.m. in many service areas, particularly in hospitals. Nursing staff and midwives seem to have a blind spot in this regard. Given that the maternity services particularly serve women then this is white sexism from a managerial point of view. Our member answered a call in the early hours in spite of being told not to attend unless on duty. While devoted to our duty we often went in fear of complicated complaints procedures and short-term contracts. Although the balance is firmly tipped against us within the organisation, for our part assistance was not denied.

ii **a co-ordinated approach** to meet and hear the needs (for women's refuges for example) being whispered quietly by women in the community. These are needs which statutory organisations have failed to meet. We were unable as a group to meet the needs of women en masse; however we were able to work with individual requests as they emerged.

iii **education for women who cannot speak or write English** because otherwise they will lack the confidence not only to gain access to services and to personal rights within their homes and communities but also to challenge the obstructive power of the white male host establishment. We Asian women are also faced with the power and control of Asian male communities – Hindu, Muslim and Sikh – who in the main utilise pseudo-religious reasons to justify

their right to control us. While women remain uneducated in general and in particular about their own religions, they will continue to be dependent upon men for interpretations which often deviate from the truth, and powerless to challenge and change these inequalities.

Twelve members of the group have done counselling courses in order to provide a listening service, followed by advocacy if needed. Three have been studying advanced counselling skills, as counsellors with appropriate language skills are hard to come by. Our backgrounds enable us to offer a non-Eurocentric understanding where appropriate. Based as they are on American models and western ideas, counselling and psychiatric services in the UK, like medicine and social work, show bias with regard to gender, class, race, religion and culture.

Grants towards running costs were applied for and encouraged initially by social services anxious to be seen to be supporting minority ethnic needs. The process ran smoothly until Asian males were allocated to oversee our applications who then destroyed our anonymity by leaking our activities to the wider community. It was now possible for people to misinterpret our group members as activists against the Asian male establishment.

Objectives of the group

- To provide equal assistance and support to all women regardless of their culture, religion or background. The group places great emphasis upon its multicultural membership.
- To celebrate the unity of womanhood and sisterhood in all its colourful manifestation and diversity.
- To respect the individuality and dignity of all women with the offer of appropriate support and assistance wherever possible.
- To promote a focus for women of all ages.
- To offer active support to women seeking access to education, employment and services as a long term goal.
- Liaison with statutory and voluntary bodies to facilitate provision of legal advice, specialist referral and intervention upon request.
- To act in strictest confidence in all members relating to clients which often includes situations of great distress and provocation.
- To provide an internal support mechanism for members as this type of work is unduly stressful and is not yet being delivered by statutory agencies.

4. ISSUES FACED BY THE GROUP

Response of Asian male professionals to the group

We were perceived as a threatening challenge to male Asian professionals such as doctors, social workers, local authority workers and teachers, offering realistic alternatives to them. Our multicultural make-up ignored religious hierarchies and disunity and challenged a concerted attack against us. Articles misrepresenting us in the white press caused Asian males great consternation and we were informed that we needed permission from them before publishing anything. Our activities therefore had to be kept discreet.

The group was attacked for trying to influence young Asian girls and described as anti-religion. Individuals, their elders and children were subjected to threats and our employers received indignant letters. The Asian professional groups mentioned above worked to create an uneasy atmosphere and sought to disband the group by underhand means.

Religion was invoked to reinforce their bogus arguments against us. Intense interrogation by elderly relatives resulted; they said good traditional women worthy of Izzat would not be involved in groups that challenged subordination. Male worshippers at the local places of worship were told to warn and keep their womenfolk away from the group; keep them at home like "all good women" was the message.

We have achieved some short term objectives while much of our work entails long term developmental goals. We were successful with some clients but, because of our personal and collective limitations, not with others. Many of us suffered burn out which led us to think that a new strategy of working with committed professionals and volunteers needed to be considered.

Attitudes of Asian male social workers

Asian male social workers are paid to adhere to equal opportunities policy but Asian female clients are not spared the male pseudo-religious ethos; they are made to feel guilty for breaking their families' privacy and their Izzat is invoked once again to make them give up seeking help and return home. Thus clients are not helped but accused of being traitors and driven away; to complain is to betray their culture.

Women who wish to leave violent domestic situations are supported by the group but likewise are encouraged to be reconciled if they wish. We do not support domestic violence but at the same time we have worked successfully as family negotiators and have recommended counselling for couples.

In these circumstances, Asian male social workers do not observe the rules of confidentiality of women's refuges and it is not unusual for these men to hunt down estranged wives and daughters. Threats of violence were issued to women members if they did not divulge the whereabouts of clients. Police tapping of members' domestic lines had to be introduced to deal with this problem.

One client involved in a court case to obtain custody of her children from a violent partner came to us in desperation. It was discovered she had been manipulated to prevent her from contacting us, and duped into signing a false statement that claimed she was mad (a valid excuse in Islamic law for divorce). She had been told that the only way she could get her children back was to sign this statement. Her brother-in-law held high office in the local authority. The male and female professionals had been working hand in glove with his family against her. The case continues as does the deterioration of the health of the client due to emotional stress and consequent serious weight loss.

Sexual harassment
Asian women in the field of employment are often assumed to be sexually available by Asian men because they have transgressed the line of respectability or Izzat. Women are still at the mercy of this kind of duplicity. Asian men are particularly aware of how Asian women are sheltered and susceptible to abuse, how they may be more naive in their communication and relationships with men. Asian women are vulnerable to blackmail; they may not be fully conversant with the reading and writing of English, and may easily be excommunicated without any lines of support if their Izzat is suspect. Their complaints of sexual harassment may be thwarted by the accused using strategies that take advantage of their vulnerability.

Asian women can be harassed within the privacy of the mother tongue, or outside office hours. The white establishment needs heavy justification for their investigation squads and the experience can be highly stressful, destructive and dangerous for the woman in the face of the wider community – they would ask why a self-respecting woman would work anyway? Out of ignorance and fear the

white professionals do not wish to interfere and any female Asian victim of Asian male sexism in such cases subsequently fails to receive any appropriate support. All this prevents Asian women from challenging sexism. Justice cannot be done unless individuals have enormous financial resources to take these issues through the legal channels. At the same time there is a serious risk to the individual and their families when insidious underhand tactics are used.

These problems have had a calamitous effect upon women just starting out and the little confidence gained has been shattered by the threatening and callous behaviour of men. These women have retreated in fear and have been put back 10 or 20 years, being told their participation in any group as women was irreligious.

Neither the women's section of the equal opportunities department nor the race section were prepared to deal with our reports of sexism; they passed the buck between themselves. Confronting Asian male officers in the authority created too much of a risk. Best to let sleeping dogs lie was the view of the local authority. As for the race section, the Asian male officers could not be seen to be overtly supporting women who were actually undermining tradition and religious practice.

The use of male violence
A vigilante service exists to assist Asian communities in finding estranged wives and daughters – and in return for a fee the Izzat or male honour of the family is restored even if violence has to be used. A number of male Asian local authority workers have colluded with this practice by obtaining national insurance numbers, making a nonsense of confidentiality on the Asian male network. The Asian language is used, while white workers remain oblivious to the confidential information being divulged. Asian males abuse their positions in this way to reinforce themselves against the white western community.

Mental health
The group believes that the diagnostic framework of psychiatry, medicine and social work is based on white male Eurocentric concepts. To be relevant to needs in a multicultural society, it should take into account the wider culture of the service user; effects of migration and resettlement for example, along with religious and other practices that offer relief. Practitioners should examine their own possible prejudices and undertake positive cross-cultural training. A recent health and local authority study has confirmed that training would make possible a change of paternalistic attitudes and raise consciousness.

One woman was told following childbirth how wonderful it was that Asian women do not suffer post-natal depression. She herself remained hospitalised and on drug therapy for six months.

Another Muslim woman from a less strict family who had married for love, was noticed with her hair uncovered by her brother-in-law without her duppata or headscarf. He exclaimed that there was a djinn or spirit dancing on her head – the djinn are said to be attracted to women's hair and perfume and this is a reason for covering up and not going out at night. Holy men were invited to offer her treatment. They sat round her in a circle and chanted prayers, telling her she had become too westernised and that she must refrain from cutting a fringe in her hair or wearing make up and she was given a silver amulet to ward off evil. The experience was desperately frightening for her and caused her hours of speculation about her own mental state. Any mental ill-health has a stigma attached and bad can come to mean mad which in turn can lead to a form of excommunication in the community. Such individuals can find themselves isolated in a no-man's land between eastern and western cultures and this is exacerbated in the case of western women who marry Asian men. The change in identity that the Asian men require can be acceptable to some, but to others it can be traumatic.

Few Asian elders are to be found in care, partly because of the strong cultural and religious values used to maintain power over their children. Although such home care indicates a high degree of dedication to duty and responsibility, the needs of the young can be denied, causing conflict.

Marriage is often a painful and anxiety-ridden experience. One client was forced into an unhappy marriage. When she left after two months and married again to escape her parents, she was told she would burn in hell for making them so unhappy and damaging the family honour which was deemed more important than her feelings.

The counselling she received from a woman youth worker at a women's activity centre was a life-line, until her husband found her a male Asian social worker who stated that the centre was run by white lesbians and that she should not attend. While his opinion was not relevant, his sexism and inability to put equal opportunities policy into practice were matters of concern. We took enormous personal and collective risk in commenting on the case. Every opportunity to help Asian women carried implications because of the attitudes of a specific

group of Asian men in the area who wished to silence dialogue. Our communication identified areas which lacked professionalism and highlighted the need for further accountability. It tended to undermine individual and collective male-oriented beliefs and power channels.

Due to a lack of communication skills on both sides and a lack of understanding of the issues at stake, services to Asian patients can often be damaging.

Many Asian women are mothers of large families and suffer from incontinence which plays havoc with the need to be clean at times of prayer. Women can be housebound because of it. Due to feelings of modesty and shame they rarely mention these afflictions to the doctor, causing them great anxiety and depression. Because the menopause is not recognised by Asian people and their doctors, mood swings and other problems are put down to madness or someone having cast a spell rather than physiological changes.

One victim of domestic violence with four children under the age of five was housed only three streets away from her husband. Not only had she lost everything but she was still in danger. Our members stayed with the woman until the local services, quite unaware of the consequences of their action, were persuaded to mobilise more support.

5. CONCLUSION AND RECOMMENDATIONS

The absence of appropriate local delivery of services has proved most harassing. We have to weigh up the personal risks against the rewards of helping those in need. There is much to celebrate in what we have achieved and in the sisterhood of all the different groups of women involved, but much more can be done.

A listening exercise needs to take place, involving not the professionals but the grass roots workers such as ourselves.

Cross-cultural training is needed for professionals.

Recruitment and selection must be made accountable and those failing to observe equal opportunities policy should be challenged or removed.

Counselling and therapy should be freely available to volunteers such as ourselves.

On-going research into service delivery and practice needs to be carried out regularly.

Sensitivity to and recognition of our own risks and achievements is needed.

Confidence in social work teams is at an all time low; confidentiality is broken in cases of adoption, violence, mental health, rape, illegitimate children and legal issues. Asian male social workers are suspected. Sexism is not being challenged adequately by Asian women, who are also victims of the male interpretation of religion; help is needed with this.

AWWAZ, its unity of women and belief in the evolution of culture, must look beyond the losses of the power struggle to the considerable achievements of its multicultural approach.

Lessons to be learned

Our group strategies have now developed from those early naive days of direct challenge into a more restrained approach to inter-group politics and power struggles. We acknowledge the part played by gender, race, class, religion and identity in the development of the Asian communities at large. Also many Asian communities have been developing with self-styled male leaders reflecting the agenda of some male Asians. While diversity has had the effect on the wider community of fostering inter-group conflict in the absence of a wider level of consciousness and responsibility in the pursuit of power, in our case *our diversity is our power*. Our one great strength is an area of wisdom arising from our religious diversity and sense of equality. Certainly this has proved to be an asset which the men have failed to master, but begs the question why the same is not possible for men, particularly those who may or may not share the same religion but certainly do share common ethnicity within our communities?

We have now adopted low key approaches geared towards helping service users in the immediate crisis and working on more educationally-based projects such as Asian Women and Sexuality. Long term goals are slower to achieve but have greater effect in educating, training and creating employment opportunities for women *in our local area*.

Chapter 5: Jewish issues in social work education

Section 1 by the Runnymede Commission on Antisemitism, the Runnymede Trust *(The extracts are reprinted with kind permission of the Chief Executive of the Runnymede Trust)*
Section 2 by Jennifer Wood

In 1995, a group of social work educators and practitioners met in Newcastle to look at ways of introducing Jewish issues into the social work curriculum. This chapter encapsulates some of the ideas that came out of the conference and considers how Jewish issues should be taught on social work programmes. Section 1 of this chapter describes briefly what is meant by antisemitism – its history and manifestations in contemporary Britain and continental Europe. It is extracted with minor modifications from a report by the Runnymede Commission *A Very Light Sleeper – the Persistence and Dangers of Antisemitism* published in 1994 by the Runnymede Trust. In section 2 Jennifer Wood addresses practice issues and suggests material which could be included in the curriculum for social work students who may work with Jewish people – (1) background knowledge, (2) Jewish identity, (3) Jewish stereotypes, (4) religion (5) community resources and (6) case studies.

SECTION 1: THE DIMENSIONS OF ANTISEMITISM

It is valuable to distinguish between three main sets of phenomena:
a anti-Judaism, i.e. hostility to the beliefs and practices of the Jewish religion;
b antisemitic racism, i.e. hostility to Jews on the assumption that they constitute a separate "race";
c anti-Zionism, i.e. hostility towards the expression of Jewish national identity which finds its focus in the state of Israel.

These distinctions have a measure of validity, in that the motivation of those who, for example, criticise or oppose Zionism may well be different from that of people who see Jews as genetically different from themselves, or who make theological or philosophical criticisms of Jewish religion. But the three kinds of discourse very frequently overlap, in reality or in appearance, and it can be difficult to disentangle them. Each is described separately in the paragraphs which follow, but with the caveat that frequently in practice they are closely intertwined.

In modern times, anti-Judaism can be based on a profound secularism and agnosticism, and its adherents may themselves have been born Jews and brought up in the faith. But also it overlaps or merges with theological critiques of Judaism made by the adherents of other religions. In its most outspoken forms it

rarely seems to be held entirely distinctly from one of the other categories of prejudice listed here. Its opposite is a readiness to learn from the insights of Jewish philosophy and theology, and from Judaism's patterns of worship and spirituality, both at the synagogue and in the home.

Modern antisemitism tends to be quasi-racial, in that it is Jews as a people who are the objects of prejudice, rather than the religion. It involves the belief that Jews are inherently and fundamentally different from non-Jews, and that this difference is genetic (racial), as well as cultural. In its extreme forms, it holds that Jews should be excluded from mainstream culture and politics, so that their participation is only on sufferance – and at the cost of their having to deny their Jewish identity and to eschew what are perceived to be dual loyalties. There are traces here of the earlier anti-Judaism, but much of modern antisemitism reflects the racialist theories of Nazi ideology and practice.

Irrespective of its origin or motivation, antisemitism has invariably involved harassment, abuse and violence against persons, buildings and symbols. This activity can be the work of antisemites organised in extremist groups or fringe political parties, but it can also be the work of groups situated in the social and political mainstream. Either way Jews are seen as threatening because of their alleged expertise, wealth, power and contacts in financial and political circles; as rootless cosmopolitans who are both unpatriotic and unreliable; as vengeful, oppressive and unforgiving.

The term Zionism has a range of meanings, both within the Jewish community and more widely. For some, for example, it is an expression of Jewish national identity which finds its focus in the state of Israel, and does not necessarily imply a particular political policy or agenda. For others, to cite a second example, it implies a vision that the land of Israel should embrace the whole of the area promised to the Jews by God in the Bible. Since Zionism itself has a range of connotations, it follows that the term anti-Zionism refers to a variety of views.

In theory at least, anti-Zionism is not synonymous with antisemitism, nor do antisemitic premises automatically or inevitably underpin an anti-Zionist position. It is not inherently antisemitic, for example, to argue that Israel should be a secular democratic state, and to oppose the principle that every Jew, and only a Jew, wherever he or she may be, has an automatic right to citizenship. It is also the case that one can hold legitimate doubts about the policies and actions

of the government of the day in Israel without being antisemitic or even anti-Zionist. Indeed, quite a large proportion of Jews were opposed to Zionism before the creation of the state of Israel, and even today there are some who remain anti-Zionist.

Nevertheless anti-Zionism is sometimes antisemitic in intention or, even when not, antisemitic in appearance and effect. The relationship between anti-Zionism and antisemitism is complicated by the facts that Israel is the only Jewish state in the world, that its establishment arose out of the ashes of the Holocaust, and that for some Jews it is seen as a divine consolation for that terrible tragedy.

Certainly antisemites often use anti-Zionist discourse as a smoke screen to hide their hostility towards Jews. This can occur on the far left as well as on the far right – in fact in any context where people are looking for a more respectable and fruitful way of expressing antisemitism. It tends to manifest itself by antisemitic vocabulary and images – in extreme cases by the use of language and terminology reminiscent of Nazi propaganda or by demonising the Israelis as Nazis, and in less extreme cases by resort to traditional antisemitic stereotyping, for example through images of the Israelis as arrogant or aggressive.

However, antisemitism is often entwined with anti-Zionism in less blatant and intended ways. Indeed, whether expressions of anti-Zionism are also antisemitic often depends on the wider context in which they are embedded. The test is whether the anti-Zionist persistently applies standards to Israel which are different from those which he or she applies to other states.

Over the centuries many distinct strands have contributed to the complex web which makes up antisemitism. They have largely been shaped by the prevailing historical, cultural and ideological currents of the time: whatever the "-ism" of the age, so to speak, the world's antisemites have never failed to latch on to contemporary political currents to provide a spurious rationale for their irrational hostility towards Jews. Thus in an age of religion, for example, religious reasons were adduced to justify hostility towards the Jews; in the age of enlightenment secular and quasi-scientific reasons were to the fore; in the nineteenth and twentieth centuries, the political doctrines of liberalism, socialism, communism, conservatism and nationalism each generated its own distinctive justifications for antisemitic hostility. Following the catastrophe of the Holocaust, when one third of the world's Jews were systematically murdered in the name of racial

purity, the creation of the state of Israel led to new opportunities for antisemitism under the cover of anti-Zionism. The latest twist in a the fable, which goes by the name of "Holocaust revisionism", seeks to deny that there was ever any systematic policy by the Nazis to exterminate the Jews of Europe. Holocaust denial seeks both to excuse and to motivate antisemitism; it originated among Nazi sympathisers, but is also nowadays to be found in extremist Muslim propaganda.

In descriptions of contemporary antisemitism in Britain, it must be understood that the full range of its manifestations is not easy to identify and that there is therefore a temptation to focus only on the more visible aspects. Moreover, particularly because of the Jewish experience of the Holocaust, and the perceived role of organised, extremist political antisemitism in its perpetration, antisemitism in the post-war world has often been described and assessed solely in terms of the strength of the far right, neo-fascist or neo-Nazi groups. In the United Kingdom there is a tendency to describe antisemitism almost solely in terms of these two factors and to ignore manifestations of antisemitism which are more deep-rooted and harmful.

Although (with the single exception currently in Tower Hamlets in East London) there are no overtly antisemitic groups or movements in the political and social mainstream, antisemitic sentiments occasionally surface in Parliament, the national and local press, and the business world. For example, during the parliamentary debates on the British legislation to prosecute war criminals, a number of its opponents betrayed unmistakable tones of antisemitism. These included assertions that the Jewish lobby was seeking to import foreign concepts of justice into the British legal system and that the Bill was the product of an Old Testament love of vengeance and should be resisted lest it inflame antisemitism. Some members of the Commons and the Lords have demonstrated an extreme anti-Zionism, which, when taken together with other less than sympathetic attitudes to Jews they have expressed over the years, appears to be an expression of antisemitism. During the Guinness affair and the accompanying trials involving a number of prominent Jewish businessmen, antisemitic undertones were detected in some of the media coverage. When the Bank of Credit and Commerce International collapsed, Jews were accused of engineering its demise because of its Islamic, Third World and Arab links. It is clear that in many circles there are those who harbour antisemitic feelings but they tend to surface mainly in connection with crises, scandals and other upheavals.

The extent to which anti-Jewish stereotypes persist and influence behaviour at various levels in society – in education, among civil servants, in the churches, the media, the school playground, the family – is very difficult to assess. One often hears the comment that most people never think about Jews and therefore are not likely to manifest any negative reaction to examples of Jews attaining high office in politics or other high profile professions. But there is some evidence to suggest that negative stereotypes may well be passed on from generation to generation: some teachers have experience of children who come to school with negative views which they have picked up in the home. There may well be disturbing levels of latent antisemitism which have no operative effect. Further research needs to be done on this. The possibility that the more hidden, covert levels of antisemitism – the antisemitism which is carried in common stereotypes the significance of which we may not fully understand – constitute a much more serious phenomenon, or set of phenomena, than organised political antisemitism, cannot be ruled out.

Heightened awareness of the problem of antisemitism in the United Kingdom stems in great part from the attention that has been paid to the resurgence of antisemitism elsewhere in Europe. Whilst Britain has never experienced the virulent strains of antisemitism which have appeared in continental Europe, there is always the fear that any increase in antisemitic activity in other European countries will find a ready echo in the United Kingdom. Given the pattern of antisemitic incidents in Britain over the last decade or so, it is clear that copy-cat incidents occur following highly publicised events on the continent.

The review by the Runnymede Commission on Antisemitism proposes six main principles:
1 Key distinctions should be made between anti-Judaism, antisemitic racism and anti-Zionism.
2 Action against antisemitism should be integrated with action against other forms of racism.
3 Antisemitism is not limited to the activities of far-right organisations, but is to do with notions and concepts of "being British".
4 Both liberal democracy and cultural pluralism need to be strengthened.
5 Identity is a key concept in all work concerned with racial equality and justice.
6 There needs to be more awareness in mainstream society of diversity within minority communities.

SECTION 2: PRACTICE ISSUES

This section looks at what could be included in the teaching relating to work with Jewish people. It is based on workshops delivered during the last few years to social workers and care staff who come into contact with Jewish service users.

I. Background knowledge
Most British Jews originate from Eastern Europe. They came to the UK in the last decades of the nineteenth and the early twentieth centuries, fleeing Tzarist persecution. Entry slowed to a trickle after the 1905 Aliens Act, which was designed to halt the perceived threat of Jewish immigration. The impoverished immigrants joined a small but well established Jewish community of merchants and traders. A further much smaller group of Jews came to the UK in the 1930s, to escape Nazi persecution. The Jewish community in Britain today comprises some 350,000 people, mainly concentrated in a few large cities. It is divided into four main groups – Hassidic or ultra-religious, mainstream Orthodox, Progressive (Liberal or Reform) and non-affiliated or secular Jews. In some ways the Jewish community is polarising. Along with the rest of society, Jews are tending to become more secular, while paradoxically, again in line with current trends, some are becoming drawn to more orthodox forms of practice.

2. Identity
Although there are great differences in practice and attitude between the groups mentioned above, it should not be assumed that one group is necessarily more pious or spiritual than another. A Progressive Jew may be more religious than someone who is nominally Orthodox but chooses not to attend synagogue regularly. Secular Jews may come from deeply religious homes and may have more orthodox relatives with whom they go to synagogue on family occasions or religious festivals. In fact, the degree of religiosity may tell us very little about the level of participation in the Jewish community. Some secular Jews express their Jewishness through the land of Israel, others by involving themselves in Jewish causes in Britain, such as charity fundraising. Some express their affiliation politically by espousing more general antiracist causes.

A Jewish woman (Guy, 1992) is quoted as saying:

> "... I have always felt that everybody who feels they have some claim on Jewish identity has an absolute right to define that in their own way." (p. 22)

On the surface few people would disagree with this saying. Closer examination, however, reveals the difficulty Jews have in defining themselves. On the one hand, the forces of mainstream Jewish orthodoxy, with the full weight of history and tradition, lay down a very clear definition of what constitutes a good Jew. Thus it tends to marginalise those Jews who do not adhere to some version of this. On the other hand, mainstream western society also has a powerful history and tradition of defining the Jew in its midst. Jewish people are often first made aware of how others regard them as different when they leave the family for the first time and start school.

In *Roots Schmoots*, Jacobsen (1993) catches some of this feeling of being trapped in other people's definitions. He remembers being reprimanded by the headteacher, along with other Jewish boys, for making a noise during school prayers:

> "... and in the pause before he threw his voice up into our bolt-holes two thousand years of theological acrimony unravelled. 'If the Jewish boys are unable to concentrate on their own prayers, would they at least do us the decency of permitting us to concentrate on ours'... " (p. 2)

This is not exactly persecution but it serves to underline differences and feelings of being apart, which at the same time is given a negative connotation.

Michael Rosen (1993) identifies a similar experience in his poem *Easter*. He describes how they were told the Easter story at primary school, including how the Jews were responsible for Jesus's death:

> "I felt a bit bad about those Jews
> I mean I didn't think Zeyde'd do a thing like that
> And I kept my head down in class
> In case anyone thought I was in on it too." (p. 14)
> *(Zeyde is Yiddish for grandfather.)*

3. Stereotypes
It is necessary for social workers to confront their own stereotypes of Jews. This helps them to recognise the factors which could impede their ability to work effectively with Jewish service users. The more pernicious cultural images picture Jews as rich, mean, money-grabbing, cunning or shrewd. Positive images often portray Jews as living in close-knit communities, as achievement oriented and as

valuing education. Jewish family values are often denigrated by the image of the Jewish mother as aggressive, domineering and guilt-inducing. As happens with any labelling process, Jews themselves come to absorb and internalise these images. The 1994 BT advertisements in which Maureen Lipman played a Jewish mother fussing over her family is a good focus for discussion. The advertisement was clearly not meant to be antisemitic, yet it generated widely differing reactions from Jewish people. One woman wrote, "I actually hate them. I think they do promote a stereotype that I'd rather didn't exist. I don't have a mother like that... I don't like that stereotype at all". Another woman expressed the opposite point of view: "I don't find that at all insulting because the stereotype of the Jewish woman, as I understand it at least, is that she cares enormously about her family and for her children. She is utterly devoted to them. Now I can only see that as a very good thing." (Guy, 1992, p. 22)

4. Religion
It is not possible to understand everything about a religion in one or two sessions, nor is it necessary to do so. Experience of working with non-Jewish staff suggests that the following represents some key areas of useful knowledge.

Life events
Social workers need to be aware of the main Jewish life events – in particular, circumcision, bar-mitzvah, marriage, death and mourning ritual.

a. Circumcision
Boys are normally circumcised when eight days old. The ceremony is performed by a ritual circumciser or *mohel*, often in the child's own home. It may be the occasion for a celebration or a more private event. This ceremony seems particularly resistant to change and many Jews who keep up little else still insist that their sons be circumcised.

Many non-Jews regard the practice as barbaric, as it is performed without anaesthetic by someone who is not medically qualified. Child protection workers have been known to discuss whether it actually constitutes child abuse. Surgeons are generally unwilling to perform this operation unless it is medically necessary. The topic clearly arouses strong feelings in both Jew and Gentile.

The social worker needs to understand that, for the Jewish family, circumcision is seen as both necessary and normal. At the same time it can be a very emotionally

charged event, especially for the new mother. Apart from the ordinary demands a new baby brings, she may have to entertain relatives and in-laws at her home, or organise sleeping arrangements and catering. She will be concerned for the welfare of the baby and may have to comfort him through a difficult day and subsequent night. In vulnerable families tensions are bound to surface at such times. Poorer families may be under additional financial strain.

b. Bar-mitzvah

Bar-mitzvah ceremonies are held when a Jewish boy is 13 (in Reform and Liberal Judaism, girls have the same ceremony). For the first time, a Jewish child takes a full part in the synagogue service and is called upon to read a long portion from the Bible in Hebrew and to take various other parts of the service. This is a considerable feat which takes many months to prepare and must be performed in front of the whole congregation and assembled family and friends. For most families it is an extremely joyous occasion and a source of great pride for parents. There is usually some form of party and the child receives presents from everybody. Social workers need to be aware of the financial pressures a bar-mitzvah can place on poorer families. For families under stress or ones which have actually broken down, a bar-mitzvah can be an added pressure. Children with disabilities may not be able to perform well, or at all, and these families may need outside help. Children in care may need to be put in touch with the relevant Jewish community if their parents wish them to have a bar-mitzvah. Clearly, children will need extra support from staff at this time especially if they are isolated from other Jewish children while in care.

c. Marriage

A wedding is usually a joyous occasion in any culture although it may also bring family tensions to the fore. In Jewish culture, it is forbidden to marry outside the faith and non-Jewish people are sometimes surprised at the hostility aroused by mixed marriages. Although many Jews today marry non-Jewish partners, Orthodox families may cut them off completely. In extremely Orthodox settings, they may even regard them as dead and ritually mourn for them. Even in more Liberal families there may be considerable opposition to non-Jewish partners and a sense of disappointment that a link in the long chain of Jewish history, culture and religion has been broken. This is compounded by the fact that in Orthodox Judaism, the child of a Jewish father and non-Jewish mother cannot be regarded as Jewish, although the child of a Jewish mother is automatically Jewish whatever the faith of the father.

d. Death and mourning

Religion requires the body to be buried within 24 hours if at all possible. Burial is followed by seven days of mourning (*shivah*). During this time prayers are said each night. The immediate relatives of the deceased remain in the house and receive comfort from family and friends who visit, traditionally bringing gifts of food. If the mourner is in residential care, social workers may need to make arrangements for people to be able to visit. If the service user wishes to visit a house of mourning at this time, social workers may need to facilitate this.

Within one year, the end of the official period of mourning is marked by a stone-setting ceremony. As tombstones can be very costly, this may cause poorer families much worry. Certainly, this ceremony can be a worse time emotionally for grieving relatives than the funeral itself, when people are often still in shock.

Social workers who work with older people need to be aware of their wishes regarding death and burial. Many Jewish people who have professed no interest in religion throughout their lives make it known at the end that they wish to be buried in a Jewish cemetery, possibly close to their parents or other members of their family. This could represent a "return to the fold" or sentimental childhood memories, or because other cemeteries are too visibly Christian with their rows of angels and crosses and flowers on the graves. Traditionally Jewish people do not use flowers: stones are often placed on the grave as a memorial. Orthodox Jews are expected to visit the graves of their dead relatives at least once a year.

Sabbath and festivals

The Jewish Sabbath lasts from sunset on Friday to sunset on Saturday. This is a time when religious Jews abstain from all work. Fieldwork visits should not be made during this time. Jews in residential homes may want to light candles and say prayers to welcome in the Sabbath or to attend synagogue on Saturdays.

Festivals are held at intervals throughout the year, such as Jewish New Year in the autumn, and Passover in the spring. It is useful for workers with Jewish service users to note the dates and have some knowledge of how they are observed. For example, the Day of Atonement is a fast day and observant Jews may not eat for 24 hours. Similarly, during Passover, Orthodox Jews may not eat bread or any products containing flour such as cakes or biscuits. Residential and day care establishments need to establish the preferred level of observance for each individual.

Dietary laws

Many people know that Jews are not permitted to eat shellfish or pork but are not aware that they cannot eat any meat that has not been prepared in a strictly kosher way, or that they may not mix dairy and meat dishes. Kosher homes have two sets of dishes and cutlery in order to keep milk and meat apart and even two sinks to wash up in. This poses a problem for service providers who cannot readily adapt their kitchens to the needs of strictly orthodox service users. In some circumstances kosher food may be brought in. If this is not possible, separate Jewish service provision may be the only option.

5. Community resources

It is sometimes difficult to understand the importance for Jews of being with one another. People cannot be part of a community on their own. The identity of an individual is constantly reflected and reaffirmed by others who share and understand common experiences. For the majority there will be experiences of antisemitism: some may share religious experiences in the synagogue, others may share memories of first generation immigrant households with Yiddish-speaking parents and traditional food and customs. Younger people share school or youth camp experience. Also because Jewish communities are relatively small, Jewish people are often related one way or another to each other, or know someone who is. This contributes to a sense of belonging.

The main UK cities have a long history of Jewish social institutions. The Jewish Welfare Board in Manchester, for example, was established in 1867. Their purpose was to help poor and destitute new immigrants. Since then Jews have been proactive in setting up communal institutions which have changed with the changing needs of the community itself. In Manchester today the range of provision includes: a team of professional social workers, a home care team, a carers team, a community centre for people with mental health problems, three Jewish day centres, three residential homes, a 65-bed home for people with learning disabilities, a Jewish housing association, Care Concern, which provides grief and loss counselling, the Jewish Marriage Council, the Jewish Blind Society and voluntary groups which provide befriending and counselling services.

Aside from social welfare provision, there are also Jewish schools, youth clubs and drama groups, as well as the communal life that revolves round the synagogues.

Such services are not available outside of large cities but, for professionals

working elsewhere, they provide a valuable resource for information and guidance. Furthermore there are cases in which an individual may choose to move back to one of the centres of Jewish population in order to take advantage of Jewish provision or to be closer to family members.

Not all Jewish service users wish to be part of the community but in working with Jewish people it remains an option to be explored.

6. Case studies

Case study 1: residential care
The first case study looks at the dilemma posed when a service user from a cultural and religious minority enters an establishment within the dominant British culture.

Ms Lee is a 22-year-old Jewish women with learning disabilities. She has lived in a social services hostel for the past three years. Before that, she lived happily with her parents with whom she retains a close relationship. She looks forward to weekends which she spends with the family at home.

Staff at the hostel think that Ms Lee is able to communicate her opinions and preferences. Her parents, however, do not agree. The staff tend to see them as over-protective and think they treat their daughter too much like a child.
Ms Lee continues to observe some Jewish customs such as lighting Sabbath candles and likes to attend synagogue once a week. Some of her customs have changed since she came to live at the hostel. At home she only ate kosher food. At the hostel she likes to join in with the other residents and now eats the same food as they do. She also goes to the pub with them on week nights and eats non-kosher bar food there.

Recently her parents observed her eating a bacon sandwich with her friends. They were extremely upset and told the staff that it must not happen again.

The staff want to encourage Ms Lee's independence and think that it is important that she begins to make choices for herself about how she wants to live.

The hostel manager wants to deal with this in an ethnically sensitive way while maintaining Ms Lee's rights.

Discussion

Most students in discussing this case tend to support the hostel staff and agree that Ms Lee is entitled to make up her own mind about what she eats. They may point out that many young people who do not have disabilities also choose to reject the customs and values of their parents. An important issue, however, is how far Ms Lee is able to make a real choice while in residential care where the dominant culture is so all pervading. At the hostel, she is also isolated from her normal family and social supports.

How far do the staff provide for her care in a way that truly gives attention to the social, spiritual and cultural well being? How far do they help her to express a sense of pride in her own identity and background? To what extent do they create a climate in which cultural and religious differences are acknowledged, discussed and valued? What steps have they taken to reduce the feelings of isolation which are often experienced by cultural minorities in social care settings? Have the staff informed themselves about Jewish culture and religion? Have they a policy for dealing with antisemitism from staff and other residents?

The other issue is that, for the Orthodox Jewish parents, the concept of choice is bogus. To be accepted by her family, Ms Lee has to behave in a certain way. This raises the issue of what "normalisation" means in this context. An ordinary Jewish life is not the same as an ordinary life in the dominant culture where a pint and a pie in the pub may be the norm. Ms Lee needs to be helped to understand the consequences of her choice of not conforming to Jewish customs. This could mean isolation from her family.

Case study 2: separate service provision

This case study looks at the justification for financing separate service provision for Jewish people. Anyborough Social Services refuses to pay for Ena Brown, a Jewish woman in her eighties, to attend a Jewish day centre. They can provide comparable but cheaper day care themselves and are willing to provide kosher food. The social worker tries to explain that Mrs Brown needs to be in a Jewish day centre for more reasons than kosher food. The care manager finds it difficult to justify the extra expense.

Discussion

The social care climate has altered radically since the implementation of the Community Care Act 1990. Social workers now have to put a very good case for

preferring one form of provision over another. This is done in writing on community care forms which set out detailed criteria of eligibility for service. In some local authorities, social workers must be prepared to argue the case orally at a care management meeting in the presence of the service user, relatives, representatives and other professionals. Although charged with offering people services which take into account social, spiritual and cultural factors, care managers have limited budgets, and also have to provide the most cost effective packages of care.

Social workers may cite the fact that Mrs Brown will be with people she knows and has grown up with; that the Jewish centre is located in a Jewish area and is geographically accessible; that the Jewish festivals will be celebrated and that she does not have to take part in the Christmas festivities. Activities may be culturally specific, for example, speakers on topics of Jewish interest or evenings of Jewish folk music and dance.

Social workers are less likely to cite institutionalised antisemitism and possible personal antisemitism. This will be a real issue for Mrs Brown. She may feel truly comfortable only with other Jewish people. If she is a Holocaust survivor and her experiences of antisemitism have been persecutory, this is even more important.

The arguments for and against the provision of separate culturally-specific services extend beyond Mrs Brown's case. If separate services are provided, this can lead to the marginalisation of those service users. It can mean that statutory services are not forced into addressing the needs of cultural minorities. It could lead to people from minority groups being directed towards culturally-specific services when their needs may be better met within mainstream services. Added to this, the uncertainty of continued funding for voluntary sector groups operating on annual grants and voluntary contributions may make people reluctant to use them in the long term. On the other hand, there is consumer demand: minority groups, including the Jewish community, continue to press for funding for their own services. Whether this is a positive demand for something more appropriate or whether it is a rejection of statutory services which fail to take account of religious, cultural and ethnic difference, remains an open question.

CONCLUSIONS

The Diploma in Social Work has done much to raise awareness among social work students on issues of race and racism in British society. This has reflected

the need to work in a way which takes account of the culture and identity of service users. For some time, however, Jewish teachers and students have been uncomfortable about the silence surrounding their own ethnicity. Responses to the silence have been mixed: some have felt there is pressure on them to identify as white and to deny that being Jewish is important; others have tried to express their experiences as Jews but have had these experiences dismissed by colleagues; still others have met direct hostility, especially in the context of the Israeli-Palestinian conflict.

Lack of awareness of Jews as a distinct religious and cultural group raises issues of equal opportunities and, in some cases, has meant that the needs of Orthodox staff and students have not been met. For example, Orthodox students report that they face difficulties in leaving placements early on Fridays when they need to be home to prepare for the Jewish sabbath; Orthodox staff members report missing key meetings because they have been scheduled on religious holidays.

Jewish service users – children and families, older people, people with disabilities – will be the ultimate losers if the social work profession fails to look at the needs of the Jews as a minority group.

REFERENCES

Guy, F. (1992) *Women of Worth* Manchester Jewish Museum
Jacobsen, H. (1993) *Roots Schmoots* Viking
Rosen, M. (1993) *You Are, Aren't You?* Mushroom Bookshop and Jewish Socialist Publications
Runnymede Commission on Anti-Semitism (1994) A *Very Light Sleeper: the persistence and dangers of anti-semitism* Runnymede Trust

Chapter 6: Reprints of articles

Continuing the series of case studies in this part we reproduce with the kind permission of the publishers four articles on various aspects of religion, ethnicity and social work which have appeared during the past decade. Selected by the editors from an extensive and growing literature as being particularly relevant to the theme of this book, they have been retyped from the original published texts with minor editing changes for ease of reading.

RELIGION AND SOCIAL WORK: IT'S NOT THAT SIMPLE! (1989)
by Paul Sanzenbach et al.
(reprinted from *Social Casework: The Journal of Contemporary Social Work*, published by Families International, Inc. November 1989)

This piece by Paul Sanzenbach written in 1989 in the United States offers a good and still relevant discussion of the problems, pitfalls and possibilities of considering the connection between religion and social work, particularly in the formation of social work values. The discussion by Edward R Canda and by M. Vincentia Joseph following the article explores the nature of the complex links between religion and social work.

Two recent articles in *Social Casework* about religion and social work,[1] as well as other publications on this topic during the past few years[2] suggest that interest in this subject area is increasing. As these authors point out, religion has been neglected by the social work profession. Despite earlier pleas for social workers to be more sensitive to spiritual issues, the profession has taken a secular stance, treating religion as a private matter with little bearing on professional practice.

Recent literature has questioned this attitude, urging practitioners to be more responsive to the needs of religiously committed clients and to recognise the spiritual dimension in practice.[3] In view of the past associations between social work and religion and the fact that social work's ethics and values have often been inspired by religious teaching, it has been argued that the expression of religious themes is not only desirable but natural.

---

1 Edward Canda, "Spirituality, Religious Diversity and Social Work Practice", *Social Casework* 69 (April 1988): 238-47; M. Vincentia Joseph, "Religion and Social Work Practice", *Social Casework* 69 (September 1988); 443-52.
2 M. Vincentia Joseph, "The Religious and Spiritual Aspects of Clinical Practice", *Social Thought* 13 (Winter 1987): 12-23; Frank M. Loewenberg, *Religion and Social Work Practice in Contemporary American Society* (New York: Columbia University Press, 1988).
3 Max Siporin, "Current Social Work Perspectives on Clinical Practice", *Clinical Social Work Journal* 13 (Fall 1985): 198-217

Indeed, it is true that social work has had a long historical association with organised religion and that many prominent social workers have been inspired by religious teaching. One need only go back to the profession's founders to recognise the link with religion, or turn to the writing of Felix Biesteck[4] to appreciate the influence of spiritual themes in the profession's literature. Despite these links, however, the claim that social work and religion are compatible needs to be more closely examined. Although religion has influenced social work, this influence has come from a *particular* religious orientation, not from religion in general. Indeed, some religious orientations are antagonistic to social work and its values and concerns.

For example, the teachings of contemporary Christian fundamentalism are in direct opposition to many of social work's commitments. Representing the views of millions of conservative Christians today, organisations such as the Moral Majority, Christian Voice, Religious Roundtable, and others have supported causes that most social workers would reject. Although some social workers of conservative opinions would endorse the New Christian Right's agenda, this agenda runs counter to mainstream opinion.

The mainstream stance of the social work profession can be contrasted with Erling Jorstad's list of fundamental moral causes:[5] the negation of choice on the question of abortion; opposition to the Equal Rights Amendment and the feminist movement in general for allegedly weakening the family; opposition to welfare and health insurance; opposition to détente with the Soviet Union and to liberal approaches to peace and international relations; opposition to homosexual rights; support for the death penalty; opposition to liberal, humanitarian values, above all to the teachings of so-called "secular humanism". Although fundamentalist theologians have not, it seems, written extensively about social work, Carl Henry's theological reflections on governmental welfare provision[6] and Jimmy Swaggart's opposition to Christian psychology and pastoral counselling[7] express attitudes that are in opposition to social work values.

Social work and fundamentalist Christianity probably disagree most strongly in the area of values. Whereas social work draws inspiration from liberal, reformist humanitarianism and is committed to individual rights, fundamentalist Christian

---

4 Felix J. Biesteck, *The Casework Relationship* (Chicago: University of Chicago Press, 1957).

5 Erling Jorstad, *The Politics of Moralism* (Minneapolis: Augsberg Press, 1981).

6 Carl F. Henry, "The State in Welfare Work", *Christianity Today* 4 (January 1960): 21-33

7 Jimmy Swaggart, "The Psychologizing of the Church", *The Evangelist* 20 (January 1988): 4-10

doctrine perceives the individual as sinful. Whereas social workers believe that professional intervention can enhance the individual's capacity for growth and change, fundamentalists would deny such a capacity, arguing instead that grace, repentance, and salvation offer the only prospect of self-actualisation and personal contentment. The social worker's belief in self-determination is also problematic to the fundamentalist, who would take a doctrinaire stand by prescribing instead simple solutions to complex problems. As Frank Loewenberg[8] has shown, the question of self-determination in the context of religious belief is complex. However, fundamentalist belief offers little flexibility. It is probable that a fundamentalist review of leading social work textbooks, journals or proceedings of national conferences and meetings would conclude that, despite the profession's good intentions, social work is hopelessly infused with the atheistic doctrines of secular humanism.

Christian fundamentalism is only one of several religious orientations that stand in opposition to mainstream social work. It is interesting to speculate, for example, how social work could be linked with the teachings and practices of fundamentalist Islam.[9] Moreover, respected Protestant scholars such as Peter Berger have become increasingly critical of the widespread use of psychotherapy as an aid to religious experience in the Protestant denominations and of their partisan support for left-of-centre political causes.[10] Catholic writers such as Joseph Sobran side with the New Christian Right on several moral issues, arguing that, although secular humanism is little more than a "minority religion", it has achieved enormous political power and should be vigorously opposed not only by Christians but by *all* religious Americans.[11]

Thus, developing a closer association between religion and social work is not as simple as it seems. Supporters of this idea do not speak for fundamentalists or indeed for religion in general but rather for a *particular* religious orientation. They are the heirs of the schism that developed between fundamentalism and the "New Christianity" in the latter half of the nineteenth century, which gave expression to the Social Gospel Movement[12] with its reformist progressivism and

---

8 Loewenberg, *Religion and Social Work Practice in Contemporary American Society*.

9 An account of the relationship of social work and Islam by Rifat Rashid is reviewed in James Midgely, *Professional Imperialism: Social Work in the Third World* (London: Heinemann Educational Books, 1981).

10 Peter L. Berger, "American Religion: Conservative Upsurge, Liberal Prospects" in *Liberal Protestantism*, ed. Robert S. Michaelson and Wade C. Roof (New York: Pilgrim Press, 1986), pp. 19-36.

11 Joseph Sobran, "Secular Humanism and the American Way", in *Piety and Politics*. ed. Richard J. Neuhaus and Michael Cromartie, (Boston: University Press of America, 1987), pp. 395-410.

12 See James Leiby, *A History of Social Welfare and Social Work in the United States* (New York: Columbia University Press, 1978).

the Religion and Mental Health School,[13] which advocated the use of psychotherapy as an aid to living and personal happiness. Although they express an approach to religion that may indeed be compatible with social work's values, social concerns, and professional commitment, their approach does not represent "religion" in general. Proponents of the view that social work should adopt a more explicit religious perspective should be aware of this fact and restate their argument to fit the complexities of religion today.

Paul Sanzenbach is Associate Professor, School of Social Work, Louisiana State University, Baton Rouge, Louisiana.

Edward R. Canda's Response

I agree with Paul Sanzenbach's principal conclusion that the connection between religion and social work involves complex issues. However, his argument requires some clarification. He cites five publications as illustrations of a revival of interest in the social work profession concerning the connection between religion and social work.[14] He seems to agree with these authors that this topic has been neglected in social work, while suggesting that these authors' calls for a close association between religion and social work are simplistic. Sanzenbach claims that these authors argue "that the expression of religious themes [in social work] is not only desirable but natural" and that "social work and religion are compatible". This view is simplistic, he alleges, because these authors ignore the fact that "some religious orientations are antagonistic to social work and its values and concerns." He uses the opposition of Christian fundamentalism to common social work values and theories of human behaviour as an example.

I agree that religious diversity, including conflict among religious people and between some religious institutions and the social work profession, needs to be examined further. However, the authors cited, including myself, do not claim that social work and religion are always compatible regarding values and beliefs. Rather, we emphasise that social workers need to understand and respond to the various religious and spiritual needs and issues in the lives of our clients and in the social environment in general. Furthermore, some (but not all) insights from

13 Allison Stokes, *Ministry after Freud* (New York: Pilgrim Press, 1985).

14 Edward R. Canda, "Spirituality, Religious Diversity and Social Work Practice", *Social Casework* 69 (April 1988,: 238-47; M. Vincentia Joseph, "The Religious and Spiritual Aspects of Clinical Practice" *Social Thought* 13 (Winter 1987): 121-23; M. Vincentia Joseph, "Religion and Social Work Practice", *Social Casework* 69 (September 1988): 443-52; Frank M Loewenberg, *Religion and Social Work Practice in Contemporary American Society* (New York: Columbia University Press, 1988); Max Siporin, "Current Social Work Perspectives on Clinical Practice", *Clinical Social Work Journal* 13 (Fall 1985): 198-217.

religious sources may be valuable for inclusion in the repertoire of social work knowledge, values, skills and practices. In order to clarify the issues raised by Sanzenbach, the remainder of this discussion will focus on three points: the conceptual distinction between religion and spirituality, the importance of taking into account religious diversity and conflict, and the position of Christian fundamentalists regarding social work.

Sanzenbach uses the term "religion" in multiple ways without defining it. He speaks of particular religious orientations, minority religion, and religion in general. This is a complicated issue, because there are many definitions of religion among scholars of human behaviour.[15] The positions of the authors he cites can be understood only by recognising the definitions that they have adopted. Each of us distinguishes between *religion*, an institutionally patterned system of beliefs, values and rituals, and *spirituality*, the basic human drive for meaning, purpose and moral relatedness among people, with the universe, and with the ground of our being.[16] Although variations exist in these authors' specific formulations, all of these authors hold this distinction in common. It helps social workers conceptualise and respond to many related aspects of clients' needs and experiences, such as moral and spiritual development, the use of prayer and ritual, the role of religious community support systems, the way in which an individual's spirituality is shaped by and expressed through diverse institutional religious forms or outside of institutional religions, and the general psychosocial functions that are served by religious forms in all cultures (so-called "religion in general"). Further, we are reminded to examine how our own diverse religious and spiritual perspectives as social workers interrelate with those of our clients. It allows social workers to be sensitive to these issues without requiring (or excluding) adherence to any single sectarian position.

These are complicated matters. Indeed, all the authors cited explicitly deal with this complexity. I examine implications of religious diversity in the three articles cited. In particular, my article dealing with religious content in social work education examines areas of potential conflict between and among social workers and clients. M. Vincentia Joseph examines functional and dysfunctional

---

15 Edward R. Canda, "Religious Content in Social Work Education: A Comparative Approach", *Journal of Social Work Education* 25 (Winter 1989): 36-45.

16 Edward R. Canda, "Conceptualizing Spirituality for Social Work: Insights from Diverse Perspectives," *Social Thought* 14 (Winter 1988): 30-46 (see pp. 41-43); Canda, "Spirituality, Religious Diversity, and Social Work Practice", p. 238; Joseph, "The Religious and Spiritual Aspects of Clinical Practice", p. 14; Joseph, "Religion and Social Work Practice", p. 444; Loewenberg, *Religion and Social Work Practice in Contemporary American Society*, p. 33; Siporin, "Current Social Work Perspectives on Clinical Practice", pp. 210-211.

religious variations throughout the life cycle. Frank Loewenberg discusses the debate between fundamentalist and other forms of religious belief and social work. Max Siporin examines areas of possible dissonance between social work and explicitly moral perspectives. Therefore, Sanzenbach's claim that we are simplistic is not justified. The importance of these distinctions and controversies needs to be accentuated.

The final point concerns Sanzenbach's characterisation of fundamentalist Christians as though they hold a uniform set of beliefs and that these beliefs are inherently in opposition to social work beliefs. Such statements oversimplify both Christian fundamentalism and social work. First, theological diversity and disagreement exist among those who describe themselves as fundamentalists as well as among those who describe themselves as social workers. Secondly, fundamentalists vary in their positions regarding social work. Some fundamentalists are professional social workers who practise explicitly Christian social work. The journal of the National Association of Christian Social Workers displays various fundamentalist and other Christian positions by professionally recognised social workers. It was fascinating to observe the diversity and disagreement among self-described Christian fundamentalists at the 1986 Conference on the Impact of Religious Fundamentalism on Social Work. Of course, there are areas of dissonance between the beliefs of many fundamentalist Christians and many non-fundamentalists, whether they are social workers or not. Fundamentalist/non-fundamentalist conflict can be heated, even violent, as illustrated recently by controversy regarding the movie *The Last Temptation of Christ* (a Christian example) and Salman Rushdie's *The Satanic Verses* (an Islamic example). Nevertheless, fundamentalists and social workers are not necessarily mutually exclusive categories and should not be stereotyped.

In conclusion, I agree with Sanzenbach that the issues involved in the connection between religion and social work are complex. It certainly "isn't that simple" – not even as simple as he portrays it. I appreciate that he raised these issues for clarification and would be pleased to see more discussion and debate about these issues in the social work literature.

Edward R. Canda, School of Social Welfare, University of Kansas, Lawrence, Kansas

M. Vincentia Joseph's Response

I agree with Sanzenbach that some religious orientations hold beliefs that are incompatible with social work's concerns, particularly cults and sects and certain fundamentalist groups. One must consider, however, that in many religious denominations in the United States, especially the mainstream religions, there are pluralistic views and interpretations of dogma or beliefs that range from fundamentalist and orthodox views to highly liberal views. Theologians and religious ethicists reflect on these conflicting views and strive through scholarly endeavours to seek the truth. Moreover, many religious denominations agree on higher, more abstract values, but hold divergent views on how these values should be implemented in concrete situations, for instance, on sanctity-of-life and quality-of-life issues. I am talking here about a pluralism that repudiates extremism wherever it is found, that not only tolerates diversity of culture, ethnicity, and religion but also values such diversity. Social workers experience a plurality of views in their profession as well.

In terms of the compatibility of social work and religion, A. P. Conrad and others have shown, historically, the integral role of the social mission of the church, for example, in the social service and social justice arenas.[17] Prior to the emergence of professional social work, many helping functions were carried out by church-sponsored or church-related groups. Today, social work remains the core profession in many church-related social service systems, such as the Catholic Charities, Lutheran Social Services, Jewish Family Services, and Baptist Ministries.

This is not to deny the challenge that confronts the professional who must deal with rigid fundamentalist beliefs. These beliefs are frequently reflected in marriage conflicts and are a source of stress for many women who are affected by rigid paternalistic attitudes and beliefs. Social workers and others are developing skills to deal with these concerns.[18] Some of these issues surfaced at the workshops on religion and social work at the 1989 Council on Social Work Education Annual Program Meeting. Both fundamentalist and nonfundamentalist practitioners and educators pointed out that consideration should be given to both strengths and challenges presented by some fundamentalist religious groups. Social workers who identified themselves as fundamentalist or

---

17 Ann P. Conrad, "Social Ministry and the Early Church: An Integral Component of Christian Community", *Social Thought* 2 (Spring 1980): 41-51; Edward T. Ryle, "Attitudes toward the Poor and Public Policy Development", in *Justice in Health Care*, ed. Margaret J. Kelly (St. Louis: Catholic Hospital Association, 1985), pp. 61-74; Brian Tiemey, *Medieval Poor Law* (Berkeley, Calif., University of California Press, 1959).
18 Robert Lovinger, *Working with Religious Issues in Therapy* (New York: Jason Aronson, 1984).

evangelical in their religious orientation emphasised the importance of their personal and professional self-awareness in dealing with clients and their respect for the client's self-determination.

My recent article on religion and social work in *Social Casework* highlights the need for social work to deal with this challenge.[19] Clearly, the practitioners in this study found religious and spiritual issues to be important to their clients and identified both functional and dysfunctional uses of religion in their lives. These issues dynamically interfaced with other aspects of the personality and the social situation. To ignore them would be to miss important and relevant treatment opportunities. Religion and spirituality are realities in the lives of our clients. In fact, polls continue to show that more than 90 per cent of the population hold theistic beliefs.

I do not agree with Sanzenbach's statement that supporters of a closer association between religion and social work are the heirs of the modernist trend that emerged from the schism between fundamentalism and the "'new Christianity' in the latter half of the nineteenth century, which gave expression to the Social Gospel Movement with its reformist progressivism, and the Religion and Mental Health School". Many supporters of the association between religion and social work would see themselves as heirs of a rich church tradition wherein services are provided to the needy. Historically, the churches have been in the forefront in providing services to the dependent, neglected, the widowed, and the elderly. Furthermore, recent evidence indicates that the shift in orientation toward the needy from an ethic of care and responsibility to a punitive stance and one of largesse were caused by the industrial revolution, the rise of the work ethic and Social Darwinism.[20] Secular humanism was rejected by certain religious denominations not because of the humanistic values it espoused but because of its rejection of theistic beliefs, which distinguished it from Christian humanism.

Clearly, Sanzenbach underlines the complexities of dealing with religion in social work. The experience of many practitioners, however, shows that many of the issues that clients bring to the practice situation are "God issues" and spiritual issues that transcend specific religious denominations and religious movements.

19 M. Vincentia Joseph, "Religion and Social Work Practice", *Social Casework* 69 (April 1988): 238-47.
20 Martin Marty, *Religious Empire: The Protestant Experience in America* (New York: Dial Press, 1970); Tierney, *Medieval Poor Law*; Ryle, "Attitudes toward the Poor and Public Policy Development"; John E. Tropman, "The Catholic Ethic vs. the Protestant Ethic: Catholic Social Service and the Welfare State", *Social Thought* 12 (Winter 1986): 13-22.

As I stated in my article and as Sanzenbach's response indicates, this is an area that the social work profession needs to address so that social workers can deal competently with these issues in practice. Some empirical exploration has been undertaken on the experience of practitioners in dealing with religious and spiritual issues with clients. Perhaps the next step should be to study socio-spiritual needs from the client's perspective.

M. Vincentia Joseph, The National Catholic School of Social Service, The Catholic University of America, Washington, D. C.

CROSSING THE DIVIDE (1990)
by Reba Bhaduri
(reprinted from *Social Work Today* 29 March 1990 and published by permission of the Editor of *Community Care*)

Reba Bhaduri argues for broadening the practice of bereavement counselling in social work. Her involvement with the dying and bereaved people from the Golborne Mine disaster made her aware of the gaps in social work knowledge base and training. In offering a transcultural approach to bereavement counselling she makes links with a spiritual and philosophical perspective.

Death, grief and sorrow have always been part of human experience. Descriptions of grief and insight into its nature appear in literature, paintings, and music of all people and times.

In several societies there are communal ceremonies and family rituals for mourning and the bereaved are distinguished by a change in their physical appearance such as special clothes, shaving hair or letting it grow and so on. The absence of such customs and rituals in contemporary Britain creates a social, psychological and spiritual vacuum for the bereaved. Yet such customs are congruent with characteristic human psychology as it offers both formal and informal support to the bereaved.

Consequence
Over the years, we have witnessed a shift from man desiring spiritual mastery over himself to physical conquest of nature. A major consequence has been that we have been impoverished in commanding spiritual and philosophical dimensions of our lives with which to transcend death. S. Radhakrishnan, an eminent Indian philosopher commented: "Modern civilisation with its scientific temper, rationalistic self sufficiency is creating a void, a ruthlessness which calls for a filling.... by the spirit of philosophy."[21]

Not surprisingly, it is often the professional or voluntary carers who bereaved people fall back on for support. Social work, which grew from a strong sense of

---

21 S. Radhakrishnan, *Eastern Religions and Western Thought*, Oxford University Press, 1939.

Judea-Christian values, has over the years shifted the emphasis from a philosophical one to one rooted in scientific thought. There is a paucity in social work literature on philosophical issues concerning the meaning of life or the spiritual purpose of life. Subjects such as sociology, psychology, the psycho-dynamic school of thought and psychiatry have made major contributions towards the growth of social work. What is not so evident is the contribution of philosophical ideas towards the growth of contemporary social work.

I feel disillusioned by the technological juggernaut of social work literature. To quote Ruth Wilkes: "The work is seen as purposive, problem solving and as having a common knowledge base derived from psychology and sociology.... This managerial approach to social work means that people are undervalued when there are no solutions to their problems, because, strictly speaking, they have no specific problems but are merely caught up in life's general misfortunes."[22]

A social work approach to bereavement which has been mostly influenced by the psychodynamic and psychological theories of loss and grief creates a sense of restlessness in social workers trying to find an answer when dealing with bereaved clients. The stance social workers take towards suffering and its significance is surely as important as an emphasis on the psyche and psychopathology of personality. Social workers may feel a sense of frustration or inadequacy in attempting to apply a prescriptive model to bereavement counselling. My involvement with the dying and bereaved people from the Golborne Mine disaster made me aware of the gap in social work literature and training which hardly prepares one to cope with such tragedies.

Research
My research on self-inflicted burns,[23] where clients wanted to commit suicide by setting fire to themselves, made me aware that my knowledge of human relationships and theories of loss, grief and of personality seemed rather inadequate, or even pretentious. I was startled to discover from several clients that their reason for attempting self immolation was to destroy their soul. It was not promoted by religious or political factors. They all seemed to have lost the meaning and purpose of life.

Britain is a multi-racial society. Given that, how often do professional and

22 R. Wilkes, *Social work with undervalued groups*, Tavistock, 1981.
23 R. Bhaduri, 'Self inflicted burns', *Social Work Today*, February 18, 1985.

voluntary carers explore and examine the racial and cultural aspects of grief and bereavement? The gap in social work literature and in training on bereavement counselling with minority ethnic groups leave social workers feeling deskilled when working with bereaved clients from these groups. They tend to withdraw from offering help.

The study on "Race and Culture in Social Service Delivery in three local authorities" by the Social Services Inspectorate, North Western Region, highlighted problems with bereavement counselling from minority ethnic groups. The study states: "... social workers felt especially out of their depth offering help to Asian families experiencing loss and grief. They said that they felt they were intruding on unfamiliar ground and were unable to interpret what was happening The tendency was to retreat feeling an outsider and then they have to cope with uncomfortable feeling that they had opted out."[24]

Alternative

My work on bereavement showed that there is a need to broaden the horizon of the traditional model of bereavement counselling. There is a need to go beyond the analytical approach to life, so that social workers will be able to communicate a sense of meaning to their clients. As there is an alternative model of medicine towards illness, there could be an alternative model in social work alongside the psychological, sociological and medical ones.

Grief is not simply a biological condition: it is a condition which demands an understanding of the entire person, including racial, cultural and religious perspectives. Should we not give as much emphasis to the spiritual dimension of life as we do to social, emotional, psychological and cognitive dimensions?

A transcultural approach to bereavement counselling attempts to make a synthesis of the existing model with the philosophical dimensions drawn from the *Bhagavad Gita* – an important landmark of Indian philosophy.

The reason for selecting Indian philosophy is that there has always been a prevalence of disease, death and suffering in India. Many things take place in the open. Death is not private, it is fully watched. Hence concern with suffering and how to cope with it has been a main theme of Indian philosophy. Every major

---

24 R. Hughes, R. Bhaduri, *Race and Culture in Social Services Delivery*, Social Services Inspectorate DofSS October 1989.

system of Indian philosophy begins with the practical problems of life and seeks the truth to alleviate pain and suffering. Philosophy is seen as an art of life and as an art of looking at life. Social work is also an art of life because it seeks truth and makes us aware of ourselves.

Relevant

Bhagavad Gita is particularly relevant to the subject of suffering stemming from life's eventualities. It offers a pragmatic way to cope with grief. As Mahatma Gandhi commented: "I find a solace in the *Bhagavad Gita*... when disappointment stares me in the face and all alone I see not one ray of light, I go back to the *Bhagavad Gita*. I find a verse here and a verse there and I immediately begin to smile in the midst of overwhelming tragedies. My life has been full of external tragedies, and if they have left no visible, no indelible scar on me, I owe it all to the teachings of *Bhagavad Gita*".[25]

Reba Bhaduri is a member of the Social Services Inspectorate.

---

25 M. Gandhi, *Young India* 1924, in S, Radhakrishnan's *The Bhagavad Gita*, London, Allen and Unwin, 1948.

OVERCOMING ABUSE: AN ISLAMIC APPROACH (1994)
by Aliya Haeri
(© 1994 *OpenMind*, Reprinted from *OpenMind* 69, June/July 1994 by permission of MIND (National Association for Mental Health))

> This article provides an applied example from a specific aspect of a religion: concept of self and change in Islam, dealing with child protection issues. It traces the path of working with users directly.

Child sexual abuse in Muslim society is not new; it is, and always has been, the unspoken taboo in all societies everywhere, occurring whenever the natural centre of the human being or of society no longer holds.

I use a counselling process for the recovery of abuse which is based on a model of the self according to the Qur'an, Islam and Sufism. This model is rooted in unity (*tawhid* in Arabic) or the Oneness of Reality. According to this model, a person is inseparable in body and spirit, mind and emotions. A person is born whole and complete, and must not be looked upon simply as a cluster of behavioural patterns, or a set of symptoms of one imbalance or other, or as a victim of abuse.

All imbalances/excesses are a symptom of the lower self; one must aspire to one's higher self if one is to avoid succumbing to the base negative tendencies. Everything in life is created in pairs of opposites. There cannot be a higher nature without a lower nature, just as there cannot be ease without dis-ease. This, simply speaking, is a law of nature. We cannot change the rule; we can only change our role. We can assume the role of our higher nature; otherwise, we will always be abused by the lower. It is by awakening to one's higher self that one avoids abuse. One can choose to live a life of quality.

In counselling cases of sexual abuse, I guide the client through a recovery process of five steps.

Step 1: Affirming the client's innocence
It is important to remember that the child is always innocent and never responsible for such acts. The responsible person is always the adult offender. Quite naturally, the child may have mixed feelings and may need to be reminded often of her innocence. Those who are closest to us often act as a kind of mirror.

We see ourselves largely according to how others see us and treat us. If the child is supported and nurtured, she is then able to accept herself as a worthwhile human being. It is this core sense of her own self-worth and self-esteem that is at the heart of her journey towards wholeness.

In Muslim communities, the taboo of sexual abuse can be so deep-rooted that the child is faced with outright denial or rejection by her family, or a blind eye is turned. A priority must be to overcome this stigma in society, by educating the public and introducing prevention strategies to encourage greater openness and support within all sectors of society.

Step 2: Release by re-living the experience

A necessary step which the client now takes in her recovery is to re-live and remember the incident of abuse. A great Muslim sage, Ali ibn Abi Taleb, said: "Wherein lies the illness, there also lies the cure." By this, we are told that the cure is in the illness itself. By allowing the abuse to surface, one has already begun to let go of it. A client may know without a doubt that she had undergone an earlier abuse, yet so deeply buried is the memory of it that she may not be able to remember. Very often, such memories may arise quite spontaneously, particularly when receiving some form of body treatment, such as massage or reflexology.

Step 3: Healing the whole person

It is not enough to counsel the client through the trauma alone, but also to treat her at the same time on the levels of the body, emotions, mind, soul and spirit, as a unified whole being.

All existence is in constant flux and change; everything is continually creating and re-creating itself. This process of constant renewal is described in the Qur'an where it says that "At every instant, reality is on a new affair" (55:29)* A person may see her body as abused; the reality, however, is that her body today is completely new, and not the one she had when the abuse occurred. This client may ask, "If this is so, why then do I still feel the effects of the abuse today? Why is there still pain and tension in the body?" The reason for this is one's memory.

If one visualises oneself as abused, the body will continue to behave as though

---

*The numbers in the text refer to the specific *surah* and *ayah*, or chapter and verse, in the Qur'an.

abused. Once the client recognises this and realises that the past is gone, she can begin to see herself in a new way. She can visualise herself as whole and in well-being. By taking this decision, she takes responsibility for her healing and creates her own reality.

The client now becomes aware of the state of her health, often overlooked over the years, and in particular the needs of her body – in terms of proper breathing, exercise and a balanced diet.

Emotions are forms of energy, and if we do not express our emotions, they become trapped and result in tension in the body. To facilitate recovery, I encourage the client to treat herself to sessions of acupressure, massage and other forms of relaxation, such as swimming and taking warm baths scented with a few drops of calming aromatherapy oils. Other useful ways of treating the emotions are Bach flower remedies, which I use, and homeopathy.

One of the first emotions to emerge may be anger, which can be dealt with in many ways. One method is a shouting exercise. The client repeats a well-known Qur'anic supplication, shouting it at the top of her voice. In Arabic, the supplication is: "*Hasbun Allahu wa ni am al wakil*". It translates as, "God is sufficient, and He is the best Guardian". The profundity in saying this is that the client is not simply expressing long-suppressed anger, but is also calling upon her higher self, her higher reality, which is the source of unity, healing and wholeness.

By combining counselling and complementary medicine, the client's inner healing and other resources may be mobilised more fully. Here, a client's own faith (*iman*) or spiritual commitment may be her most invaluable resource. We all seek meaning and purpose to our existence. Our purpose in life gives value to our existence as human beings while it motivates us to transcend our limitations in reach of a higher reality. One's faith and trust in God may serve as an unswerving pillar of strength at a time when the recovering client is seeking a foundation of certainty in her recovery.

The Islamic *salat* (ritual) prayer is a source of grounding; performing the prayer regularly five times a day can provide the client with an ongoing sense of order and steadfastness, giving her a sense of continuity over time. The ritual ablution of the *wudu* (the washing of certain parts of the body) and the *ghusl* (the washing

of the entire body) before prayer also help to serve as a continual source of cleansing and purification, and this is especially true if one's intention (*niyyat*) to perform it is sincere. With a pure intention, one feels both an outer and an inner cleansing – a washing away and purifying of the body as well as of the heart, mind and soul.

Apart from the ritual prayer (*salat*), the client may discover her own inner strength through supplication (*du'a*) and invocation (*dhikru'llah*) of God's Beautiful Names and Attributes, as well as other spiritual recitations. The reading of the Qur'an and studying its rich and deep meanings help to enlighten our outlook and uplift our hearts. The Qur'an is a divinely revealed book which can be read on many levels; at its most profound level, it speaks to our highest inner reality. Its words can revitalise and awaken hearts, giving new life and renewing the human spirit. The chapter entitled "The Beneficent", (*Surat al-Rahman*), is considered especially to be a source of healing.

Ultimately, the quickest way to overcome a negative experience is to take on a new commitment of positive action. For a person of faith and trust (*iman*), immersing herself in positive action is a transformative step. It can be the surest ways of shifting her energies into life, and leaving behind the nightmare of her past.

Step 4: Empowering the client to see justice done

The client, once helpless, now has the power to act to see justice done. She is empowered with genuine options, and can choose to do nothing, or to divulge the identity of the offender(s), to confront the offender with exposure of his criminal acts, or to take legal action against the offender.

Of greater importance to the client may be the need to reconcile her relationship with her parents and to come to terms with the question: why did they not protect her? A child's security in this world is based on a relationship of trust with her parents. So deeply rooted is this trust that the Qur'an admonishes the believers to not betray that which is entrusted to them (8:27). If the parents are no longer alive, the client may find certain visualisation exercises provide a deeply intuitive means of contact with her parents. Because the believer knows that all life does not die but survives in an ongoing eternal state, the visualisation can be very powerful and often takes on a reality of its own, helping the client confront and understand the parent.

Step 5: Liberation through unity

Ultimately, the client's freedom comes from a perspective of unity. By seeing the total picture, the client begins to grasp the interplay of the people and circumstances which unfolded around her, which led to her being the person who was abused. This may help the client to view the incident in its total perspective, hence enabling her to eventually find herself capable of forgiveness in the sense of letting go.

In conclusion, the life of this world is such that there will never be an end to the abuses. No sooner is one healed by this abuse, than one turns to be struck by another. Ultimately, the only true ease and freedom comes from a trust and faith – by turning to the aspirations of the higher self, of a higher reality.

This is the destiny of all human beings and what it means to be truly human. The Qur'an says, "Surely you are of a tremendous nature" (68:4). If abuse can turn us away from the limitations of our existence and towards the mercy and healing of a higher reality, which is also within, then we have learned that the purpose of this life is to awaken us to our inner potential, to our higher self, and to the One Supreme Reality.

This is an abridged version of Aliya Haeri's speech at a seminar organised by Amana Project.

SOCIAL WORK, SECTARIANISM AND ANTI-SECTARIAN PRACTICE IN NORTHERN IRELAND (1996)

by Marie Smyth and Jim Campbell
(Reprinted from *British Journal of Social Work*, 1996, Volume 26, pp. 77-92)

This paper provides a basis for examining antiracist and anti-discriminatory practice in relation to levels of subordination (unexplained) and its relationship with the state. Issues raised in training social workers for anti-sectarian practice are pointed out without defining sectarianism. It also discusses training for anti-sectarian practice, based on the authors' analysis of social work and sectarianism. We suggest that this article should be read together with Brewer, J. (1991) 'The Parallels between Sectarianism and Racism' in CCETSW (1991) *One Small Step towards Racial Justice – the teaching of anti-racism in Diploma in Social Work programmes* London: CCETSW.

Summary

This paper addresses a subject relatively unknown to the British and international social work audience – that of training for anti-sectarian practice. In doing so, it points to some of the complex, even dangerous issues raised by such training for social work students and practitioners in Northern Ireland. The paper comments upon the limited but significant ways in which social work educators and practitioners have tried to challenge sectarian discrimination in Northern Ireland, and proposes methods in training and research which might facilitate a better understanding of these processes.

Introduction

Thompson (1993, p. 137) suggests that, "whilst Northern Ireland is a good (*sic*) example of sectarianism, the concept is, of course, far more widely applicable on a national and international basis than simply within the province". There are indeed lessons to be learned by other social workers given the experience of their colleagues in Northern Ireland, but the peculiar fact remains that, despite the intensity of research on the conflict during the past 20 years (Whyte, 1991), little has been said about how social work has been affected by "The Troubles". In engaging in this debate we wish to:

● indicate why we believe Anti-Racist and Anti-Discriminatory Practice (ARADP) is important in assisting social workers and social work students address various levels of subordination in society;

● explain how an understanding of ARADP can help us analyse the role of social work and its relationship with the state and sectarianism in Northern Ireland;
● propose ideas for training and research for anti-sectarian practice.

Social work in the 1990s: The case for **ARADP**

One outcome of ARADP training for UK social workers has been an acknowledgement of the prevalence of structural, institutional and personal forms of discrimination in society (Central Council for Education and Training in Social Work (CCETSW), 1991, 2.2.3), and the need for social workers to be trained to be pro-active in identifying and addressing various forms of disadvantage. This approach is a departure from the professional stance represented in the earlier Code of Ethics (British Association of Social Workers (BASW), 1975), and fits more easily with the radical social work literature which emerged around the same time (Leonard, 1976; Corrigan and Leonard, 1978; Bolger *et al* 1981; Simpkin, 1989). The Code of Ethics, however well-meaning, suffers from what Clarke and Asquith (1985, p. 87) describe as having "only a vague and distant relationship with any discernible moral doctrine". The Code espouses, for example, such complex principles such as "respect for persons", "individuation", or "confidentiality", without fully acknowledging their close association with wider personal, professional and political ideologies. This has often encouraged educators and practitioners to assume that such principles are self-evident: politically and socially neutral.

The paradox of this conventional wisdom is that these principles help to formulate a specific vision of the world which professionals may feel comfortable with, but one which can guide social workers towards practices which impinge on the rights of their clients (Rojek *et al.*, 1988; Biehal and Sainsbury, 1991). These ethical principles, far from being rational guides to professional behaviour in the context of "objective" social relationships are, in fact, contestable (Gallie, 1955; Campbell, 1986). They incorporate contentious social concepts which are meaningful largely in terms of the ability of particular interest groups (in this case social workers) to interpret their view of the social world at the expense of rival formulations (clients'). The emergence of the idea of ARADP has allowed the profession to move beyond the pseudo-neutral statement of values and towards a more open acceptance of the inevitability of ideology in social work practice. In particular, there is now an enhanced recognition of the complexity of social disadvantage and how oppressive structures condition the language and practice of the profession.

Expressed in this way, ARADP can be seen not as a totally novel idea, but as part of a history of ideological conflict in the practice of social work. This is a history of recurring tensions in role and function, between neutrality and partiality, the personal and the political, individual agency and structural determination (Clarke, 1993). The emergence of ARADP has allowed the profession to begin to reinvestigate the relationship within and between such dichotomies – which exist, in any case, regardless of inspection. What this debate can offer is the opportunity for social workers to discuss relationships of power which exist between themselves, their clients and the state, in a way which was stifled by assumptions about core values. Thus the discussion moves beyond the traditional concern about "good" and "bad" practice (and consequently about "good" and "bad" social workers), towards the more complex, symbiotic relationship between the profession and the society it serves. It remains to be seen how much that society wishes social workers to engage critically with social problems and issues of social justice.

The case for ARADP is strengthened by an examination of how the social work profession has tried to deal with wider social pressures when they have impinged on the value base of the traditional casework relationship. For example, the tension between the aspiration to care for clients, and the controlling function prescribed by law and employing agency, exposes the interface between the benign hopes of practitioners and the realities of relative powerlessness experienced by many clients. Such contradictions arise because social workers habitually mediate in the relationship between the state and citizens over rights to goods and services. A consistent historical function of social work since the Poor Law has been that social workers perform a gatekeeping role in the distribution of these resources. Now, as then, the nature of this function is acutely manifest in times of relative economic scarcity, when concepts of deserving and undeserving poor re-emerge (Jordan, 1990; Becker and MacPherson, 1988; Davis, 1991). Given that, with few exceptions, social work clients emerge from the most deprived and disadvantaged sections of society, it is inevitable that substantial numbers of "cases" seen by social workers have experienced, or been subject to, discrimination of one kind or another. The emergence of the concept of ARADP has facilitated the examination of discrimination in society, encouraging analyses of social work interventions which might be effective in challenging disadvantage.

These changes to training and practice have not been without discomforts.

Trivialising ARADP work is *de rigueur* in some circles, reinforced by the current debate on "political correctness" (Pinker, 1993; Appleyard, 1993; Phillips, 1993; Harwin, 1993; Hugill, 1993). Yet contemporary analyses of social work with women, ethnic minorities and disabled people (Dominelli, 1988; Hanmer and Statham, 1988; Oliver, 1991) suggest that there is a need for the profession to grasp the concept of the all-pervasive nature of certain forms of subordination, without spiralling towards the absurdly reductionist position which critics of ARADP accuse the profession of taking. Recognising and challenging sexism, racism, and, in Northern Ireland, sectarianism, is a complex and demanding task for any professional group or agency. As Husband (1992) has pointed out, because it is an area in which social work has been at the forefront, there are few reference points to use as guides when difficulties in practice occur. Social workers find it easier to understand the problems of the individual and to achieve change at the personal and familial levels, whilst often ignoring powerful structural and environmental factors. Through ARADP, social workers have the opportunity to begin to address these more profound levels of disadvantage, and with this realisation, construct small but significant ways of challenging the *status quo* in the groups and institutions which are powerful sites of resistance to change.

It would be a great pity, particularly for social work in Northern Ireland, where we have not experienced the same levels of resistance to training for ARADP as elsewhere, if there is any retrenchment on the ARADP requirement. Further research on and analysis of the difficulties and achievements of ARADP is required, and the development of guidelines on good practice is called for. Otherwise there is a danger that the achievement of ARADP work will be lost. It is hard to see how social work as a profession, which works with clients whose lives are most dramatically affected by oppression and subordination, can countenance a situation where it can be seen to be back-tracking on a commitment to challenging racism and other systems of subordination at a time when racism, particularly, is growing in various corners of Europe. The ARADP training requirement has legitimated attempts to address problematic issues, and has contributed to a heightened awareness, and a healthier, if more difficult, agenda within the profession. Anything less than a requirement would not have stimulated a debate about sectarianism and social work in Northern Ireland. The argument below is that this impetus, particularly in the area of training, faces resistance in agencies whose policies and practices are at best non-discriminatory, at worst compatible with the reproduction of sectarian division.

The state, sectarianism and social work in Northern Ireland

The experiences of social workers in Northern Ireland are at times comparable, yet often dissimilar, to those of their English, Scottish, Welsh and Southern Irish counterparts. The high levels of poverty and disadvantage which occur throughout these islands "can reinforce the oppression experienced by the poor in our society. It can give rise to clients' responding and behaving in ways which confirm the social worker's view that they are 'helpless', 'hopeless' or 'dangerous'" (Davis, 1991, p. 88). Other unequal divisions of gender, race, disability, sexuality and age are present in Northern Ireland as elsewhere. It is the added dimension of sectarianism which makes ARADP training and practice so difficult and yet so crucial in Northern Ireland. As with other systems of subordination, we cannot understand the everyday, lived experiences of practitioners and clients, if we do not consider the historical determinants of discrimination and the factors which help explain its persistence in personal, social, political and cultural forms. We argue that the relationship between social work in Northern Ireland sectarianism can best be explained with reference to the development of the state. Sectarianism is a product of the particular formation of the state in Northern Ireland and is manifest at institutional and ideological levels as well as in popular culture, interpersonal attitudes and behaviour. Sectarianism is culturally reproduced within the context of the particular formation of the state, which creates and maintains conditions permissive of its reproduction. This analysis is a necessary prerequisite for anti-sectarian practice, and consistent with the view that personal social work practice has a mutual relationship with these wider social structures (Brewer, 1991).

As a relatively impoverished part of the UK, the citizens of Northern Ireland traditionally have experienced high levels of social and economic deprivation (Ditch, 1983; Ditch and Morrisey, 1992; Gaffikin and Morrisey, 1990; Evason, 1985; Teague, 1993). A variety of explanations for the persistence of adverse social and economic conditions are provided – the consistent failure of the economy, even in periods of relative economic growth, to sustain sufficient employment; the inadequacy of attempts to attract and maintain inward capital investment at a time when traditional industries were in terminal decline; the inherent instability of a state which, from the outset, failed to establish equal rights of social, economic and political citizenship for all its members. High levels of public expenditure, at least until the early 1990s, can be understood as some form of response to these failures. These were the conditions in which sectarianism was fomented and which shape the nature of the existing conflict in Northern Ireland.

It is inconceivable that, somehow, social work could be detached from these relationships. Sectarian discrimination provided the rationalisation for the removal of responsibility for personal social services provision from local government in 1972. It was then that, following allegations of discrimination against Catholics, that most local government powers were allocated to quasi-autonomous "non-sectarian" government bodies (O'Dowd *et al.*, 1981; Connolly, 1990; John, 1993). Education is now administered through four education and library boards, housing through the Northern Ireland Housing Executive, and health and personal social services through four health and social services boards. These structures created opportunities for relatively high public expenditure and the development of professionalised services. But the costs were high – the loss of democratic accountability and the tendency to pursue technocratic, over-professionalised solutions to political, social and economic conflict.

To suggest, therefore, that the differences between social work in Northern Ireland and Britain are differences of content rather than form is to ignore this past. Given the problematic history which preceded their establishment, these bureaucracies were conceived and organised to deliver services which were somehow detached from the discrimination which existed in the society generally. With hindsight, the attempt to solve discrimination simply by removing powers from local government and placing them in the hands of what Rolston (1983) calls "technocrats" was naive. Our current understanding of the complex processes of discrimination and subordination, and the inadequacy of equal opportunity policies alone to redress imbalances in rights, rests on insights which have all been developed in the period since 1972.

Despite this critique, and perhaps because of the imperative to be seen to be "removed" from the conflict, government agencies have not acknowledged their association with sectarianism. There is a predictable institutional resistance to exploring openly the influence of sectarianism in the delivery of social services, given that the rationale for the creation of these structures was to eradicate these biases. To embark on such a project is to admit the possibility that the rationale for restructuring social services over 20 years ago was misplaced and that the goal which underpinned that restructuring has not been achieved. It also raises the crucial issue about how reformable the state can be (O'Dowd *et al*, 1980). Yet these questions are infrequently raised in discussions which social work students and practitioners have about their role in this society. Social workers, employed directly or indirectly by the state, work with clients who are generally the poor

and disadvantaged sections of the society and arguably the most acutely affected by "The Troubles". Given our analysis of the state and civil society in Northern Ireland, we ague that social workers cannot avoid being drawn into the conflict. In early interpretations of how the violence affected personal social services, Darby and Williamson (1978) and Griffiths (1978) noted the way in which social workers and employers attempted to distance themselves from the issues which were creating conflict, often having to accept a transfer of their powers and functions to paramilitaries and community groups. Bamford (1981), on the contrary, has described how services were delivered effectively in the midst of the turmoil, because, he argued, social workers remained and were perceived to be somehow detached and above the conflict. Bamford's position broadly represents the non-sectarian stance which, in spite of the current emphasis in training on ARADP, many social workers continue to take.

Sectarianism has an impact at different levels of service delivery in Northern Ireland. For example, agency policy is often designed to follow the contours of sectarianism. Residential child-care provision, parallelling the segregation of the educational system, is organised largely around the religion of the child and his or her parents. Whilst recognising the rights of clients to have choices in services, in Northern Ireland the rationale for the organisation of facilities is often less worthy, mostly based on the convenience of not confronting sectarian divisions. Similarly, day-care, even hospital services, frequently cater for exclusive sections of the community, particularly in Belfast, where geo-political boundaries determine the accessibility of facilities for each community (Boal and Douglas, 1983).

If sectarian criteria contaminate agency policy-making, it is hardly surprising to find social workers adjusting their practice to fit this threatening environment. Social work interventions which would seem peculiar, if not irrational, elsewhere, become commonplace and slip unremarked into the culture of practice in Northern Ireland. Such difficulties become apparent, for instance, when mental health and child protection social workers are dealing with situations of risk, whilst carrying out statutory duties. Although such circumstances might be familiar to all social workers throughout these islands, the conflict in Northern Ireland creates its own fears and anxieties for the practitioner. Police involvement in such instances is complicated by the need for an army presence (in some areas) designed to protect the police. This makes a difficult, traumatic situation more stressful for clients and social workers. Whatever the level of skills and experience of the social worker, the extraordinary conditions of work created by

civil conflict have considerable implication for personal safety and professional practice (Bamford, 1981).

This practice is also shaped by the vagaries of social policy which is either designed specifically for Northern Ireland, or is UK policy functioning to "suit" local circumstances. One example of this was the *Payment of Debts Act* (DHSS, 1976), a piece of emergency legislation which gave agencies powers to deduct state benefits at source. The Act was originally constructed to undermine a rent and rates strike organised to protest against the introduction of internment without trial, but it was subsequently used for other "non-political" purposes – to collect electricity arrears and other domestic debt. The legislation was draconian; there was, for example, no appeal procedure against arrears recovered from state benefits. Some social workers responded by using section 164 of the *Children and Young Persons Act* (DHSS, 1969) to alleviate pennilessness created by such legislation (Rolston and Smyth, 1982). (The DHSS eventually introduced guidelines to regulate the operation of the *Payments for Debts Act*.) There was a similar response by other social workers in relieving fuel and poverty shortages during the Ulster Workers' strike in 1974 (Boyle, 1978). In both examples the profession selected "caring" legislation to justify the amelioration of the conditions created by sectarianism.

There also have been discernible attempts by social workers, throughout the period of the Northern Ireland conflict, to influence events and maintain independent judgement despite the pressures to withdraw to the protection of bureaucratic policy. Early on in the conflict probation officers decided not to become enmeshed in court-directed assessments of those accused or convicted of politically motivated offences (Kelly, 1979), and the service has devised ways of positively working within the contradictory pressures created by "The Troubles" (Chapman and Pinkerton, 1987). Collectively, social workers have also used their trade union, the Northern Ireland Public Service Alliance, to join with other trades unionists to campaign against sectarianism. The Northern Ireland Congress of Trades Unions has latterly devoted resources to anti-sectarianism, notably towards the founding of an anti-intimidation unit, *Counteract* (Wilson and Wright, 1992).

Recent attempts have been made to confront the issue of ARADP by at least one health and social services board (Eastern Health and Social Services Board, 1992), but, perhaps for the reasons outlined above, it has been the voluntary

agencies in Northern Ireland which have taken the lead in developing anti-sectarian practice (Brewer, 1991; Logue, 1992). Until the more recent effects of social policy, post-Griffiths, voluntary agencies have not so readily been identified with the state, and the technocratic project which coincided with "direct rule". Traditionally they have been more likely to be closer to the communities they serve, even if their personnel have not always been drawn from these communities. This would suggest that their staff may not have been so infused with the ideology of professional detachment which affects social workers employed by health and social services boards. As a result the voluntary sector has generated policy statements on anti-sectarianism, codes of practice and training initiatives. It is not clear, however, that voluntary agencies can maintain this critical edge if the direction of current social policy continues to push them and their workers towards the sorts of bureaucratised functions which have restricted the development of anti-sectarian practice in public bodies.

These attempts to address sectarianism, at practice and collective levels, remain piecemeal and relatively unusual, but nonetheless encouraging to the ARADP training project identified earlier. The remaining discussion will focus on the way in which training for anti-sectarian practice, and research into training, can make a positive contribution towards addressing this form of discrimination in Northern Ireland.

Training and research into training for anti-sectarian practice

For some time at The University of Ulster at Magee, Derry, and more recently at The Queen's University of Belfast, training for anti-sectarian practice has been developed, influenced by our analysis of social work and sectarianism as expressed earlier in the paper. In an average class of 40 postgraduate students, many accounts of the effects of sectarianism emerge. Classes sometimes contain, for example, ex-prisoners convicted of politically-related offences, or daughters or sons of policemen killed in the last 25 years. At times students and staff have lost homes, jobs, or even their self-respect as a consequence of the conflict. There is an understandable initial fear amongst students of what will happen if secrets and feelings are revealed, mirroring the general distrustful malaise which pervades Northern Ireland. How much of that fear is based on material risk of violence, however, and how much is a form of resistance (which is an essential part of the maintenance of sectarianism), is a question which requires to be addressed. A starting point for training for anti-sectarian practice, given these powerful anxieties, is the need for trainers and trained alike to accept individual

responsibility whilst acknowledging the structural causation and institutional sustenance of sectarianism. Successful participation in the training requires a faith in the possibility that positive change can occur, an ability to control anger, and a capacity to express and tend to hurts caused by subordination. It also requires tolerance and understanding of each others' mistakes, an ability to listen to anger and hurt without being reactive, and many other skills which we as social workers recognise when used in other places. Yet the application of these skills to discussions on sectarianism presents a real challenge to staff and students alike, because we are dealing with fearful issues which impinge upon our very identities, in a society where those identities are frequently threatened.

There are a number of ways of establishing trust in these crucial early stages. We have found it important, for example, to try where possible to co-lead with trainers from the "other" religion. As part of this process, we self-disclose about our own identity and background, our growing up with sectarianism, and the problems we have in confronting the dangerous issues of Northern Irish society. This modelling is followed by the forming of a contract under which students are expected to respect ground rules on listening to and respecting others' opinions and agreements about self-disclosure. Creating an atmosphere where people are able to speak in relative safety is paramount, because there is a sense of physical danger. Students are asked to work in pairs or small groups, discussing how they have personally or professionally experienced sectarianism, yet they are made responsible at all times for their own self-disclosure or non-disclosure and the management of attendant risks. Such interpersonal exchanges, often with peers from "the other community", are an important but not sufficient basis for developing anti-sectarian practice. The inclusion of inputs and discussions of theories about sectarianism, social work and the state in Northern Ireland is crucial in moving beyond the personal and interpersonal and towards an understanding of the structural causes of subordination. A model for practice at these different levels is introduced. Finally students are asked to integrate these experiences, and move towards identifying strategies for anti-discriminatory practice (Smyth *et al.*, 1993).

Research on ARADP and anti-sectarian practice is at an early stage. In a pilot study of a first year group of approximately 50 students starting the Masters in Social Work course at The Queen's University of Belfast, it emerged that Catholics outnumbered Protestants approximately 2:1, an inverse of the ratio to be found in the general population. It is widely recognised in the profession that more members of the minority Catholic community apply for social work courses,

are recruited and therefore become employed as social workers in Northern Ireland. The reasons for this phenomenon are probably complex – and may include such factors as accessibility to third level educational opportunities in the social sciences, and the perception that social work may be a more permissible or available form of state employment that others – the police or medical profession, for example. The full implications of these determinants are worth further examination in future research.

As a way of testing their beginning knowledge base, students were asked to speculate about which theories might explain the conflict (for example, Marxist, nationalist, unionist), and what their understanding was of how government and social work agencies challenged sectarianism. Students expressed a variety of causal theories about "The Troubles", and were reasonably knowledgeable about anti-discriminatory legislation, but had only sparse awareness of how social work agencies attempted to deal with sectarianism. Further work will include longitudinal survey of how students' knowledge bases are affected by college and practice-based curricula over the two-year period of professional training.

In a more substantial piece of research which focused on how students on two social work courses at The University of Ulster, Magee College, met the ARADP requirement on practice placement, significant differences emerged in perception and training between students and their assessors (Smyth *et al.*, 1993). Low levels of ARADP training in field supervisors, tutors and internal examiners were found, and it was often the case that the student had more ARADP training than any of these other groups. In spite of the difficulty which some respondents reported in defining some forms of discrimination, in interview they appeared to be able to identify discrimination in practice, and to begin to engage in anti-discriminatory practice. Some practice teachers reported feeling less knowledgeable than students whilst others had completed ARADP training as part of their Practice Teacher Accreditation training, and therefore felt somewhat more comfortable in engaging in these processes.

The research found that a high percentage of students presented evidence of anti-sectarian practice. This could suggest that sectarianism is emphasised in the teaching. Alternatively, the research points out that perhaps the work reflects the personal commitments, concerns or individual histories of students. The findings catalogue the volume of anti-sectarian work presented by students, reflecting the interests or influence of the students' practice teachers; one practice teacher who

was interviewed saw the student as an ally, making it possible for her to work on issues she otherwise could not address. Agency policy on sectarianism and the "sectarian climate" in the agency were major influences on anti-sectarian work. One practice teacher in the study commented that sectarianism was a disablement specific to Northern Ireland, and saw it as both "physically disabling (restricting movement) and mentally/emotionally disabling (because of fear, hopelessness and so on)". The survey also revealed a lack of clarity and consistency in definitions of sectarianism given by respondents. Students' work contained implicit recognitions that there were sectarian divisions in Northern Ireland and that these divisions were problematic. However, the nature of the problem, and its implications in any broader sense, were rarely explored by students.

The research examined several pieces of evidence of anti-sectarian work, two of which focused on religious belief and religious practice, and the importance of respecting rights to religious practice. In spite of the sensitivity attached to these issues in Northern Ireland, and the difficulty in raising these issues with clients or colleagues because of the culture of silence and denial, the research suggested that these types of issues were perhaps amongst the easier ones to raise in relation to sectarianism. The study concluded:

> Where the issue of paramilitary involvement arose, the stakes became higher. One student who was working with a client who was under threat for drug dealing from a paramilitary organisation felt unable to allow the interview for this research to be taped. A second student who had a personal tragedy in his/her past which was related to "The Troubles" was highly anxious about the confidentiality with which the evidence of practice would be treated. In such a situation it is difficult for students to produce evidence of their personal or interpersonal work, where to reveal certain information about oneself or others feels and is risky. Yet the content of the evidence presented on sectarianism does not explain this fear. There is little reference to intimidation, shootings, kneecappings, bombings or talking to paramilitaries, or the security forces. There is some reference made to the impact of residential segregation on clients' lives or on students' experiences of going into certain areas. But one still has a sense of a great silence, in which unspeakable things are dealt with, they are the more fearful because of the silence which surrounds them and the resulting isolations in which they must be managed.
> (Smyth *et al.*, 1993, p. 49)

Sectarianism was the second most frequent issue presented in ADP evidence,

according to the study, yet there was some dissatisfaction with this. Some practice teachers and practice assessment panel members were not satisfied with this and asked for less emphasis on sectarianism. Interestingly, the research points out that nowhere in the course guidelines or requirements are students specifically required to produce evidence on sectarianism, as opposed to other forms of oppression, yet some agency personnel and practice teachers thought that sectarianism was emphasied more than other issues and were unhappy with this.

The research also noted geographical differences within Northern Ireland, explaining some of the difficulties experienced in undertaking work on sectarianism, which seemed to be more intense in certain locations than in others. The Greater Belfast area, the eastern regions of Northern Ireland generally, and mid-Tyrone, seemed to experience an atmosphere of more intense fear than elsewhere. The study attributed this to the distribution of sectarian violence within Northern Ireland at this time. Those working in rural areas also expressed more fear about addressing sectarianism, related in at least one instance to the isolation in which the work was carried out. It was in the work on sectarianism that the most obstacles seemed to be encountered. In one case where the student was not given permission by the practice teacher to raise the issue in the office, the situation was rationalised by the argument that to raise the issue of sectarianism was perceived as "upsetting relationships". We know from our own experience that this is not an isolated case, but is widespread in social work offices (and elsewhere) in Northern Ireland. To raise the issue to disturb a silence which has been maintained for a long time on issues related to sectarianism. Sometimes whose who raise the issue are themselves accused of "being sectarian", such is the strength of the resistance to engaging with the issue. Yet further work on the management of that resistance, and learning more effective ways to engage with sectarianism, seem more urgent now than ever, as we and our clients live in a situation where peace is being talked about, yet sectarian violence continues and the segregation between the two communities deepens.

Conclusions
The implications of ARADP for training social workers in Northern Ireland are many. It seems to us that effective ARADP work requires of social workers the ability to tolerate conflict and ambivalence. Advanced skills in working with resistance, our own as well as those of clients, colleagues and professional organisations, are also required. This shared experience suggests that ARADP training and practice can unleash enormous quantities of anger in clients,

colleagues and ourselves. The ability to work constructively with anger is central to success. In ARADP training and practice we encounter resistance, avoidance, denial, fear as well as excitement, empowerment, growth and learning.

Furthermore, ARADP training demands a knowledge of how change occurs at structural as well as individual levels. This should be made easier by the fact that the profession is grounded in the disciplines of social science which increasingly have become engaged in documenting the effect on people of exploitative treatment at the hands of systems, institutions and individuals. The argument presented is that social workers cannot work with the dynamic and effects of exploitation yet remain equivocal about its continuity. In order to acknowledge these processes, the profession must engage with the issues of injustice which confront every social worker.

The longer term ramifications of social work's involvement with ARADP remain to be assessed. We argue that the integrity of social work's contribution to the society it serves, and its ability to form part of the solution to social ills, depend on the profession's readiness to allow strategies such as ARADP to continue.

Darby and Williamson, writing in 1978, argued that in Northern Ireland, "the political nature of social work involvement is often unrecognised or misunderstood. It is virtually impossible for any field worker to maintain a consistently non-political stance" (Darby and Williamson, 1978, p. 94). Fifteen years on, the social work profession in Northern Ireland remains largely captivated by an ideology of benign detachment, one which fails to address the insidious effects of sectarianism on practice. More than ever, training for anti-sectarian practice offers opportunities for social workers to address division, conflict and injustice in Northern Ireland, and to design and consolidate professional strategies which avoid collusion with sectarianism and at best offer some positive alternatives in the context of a society urgently in need of such choices.

Marie Smyth lectures in the School of Social and Community Studies, the University of Ulster, and teaches at the Smith College Graduate School of Social Work, Massachusetts. She is currently engaged in action research on segregation in Northern Ireland, as well as researching the long-term physical and emotional effects of "The Troubles" in Northern Ireland. Jim Campbell lectures in the Department of Social Work, The Queen's University of Belfast. His doctoral thesis was on the concept of violence in social and political thought. His current research interests include social policy in Northern Ireland and mental health social work.

REFERENCES

Appleyard, B. (1993) 'Why paint so black a picture?', *The Guardian*, 4 August 1993

Bamford, D. (1981) 'Lessons for learning when the home fires burn', *Social Work Today*, 12, 47, pp. 8-9

Becker, S. and MacPherson, S. (1988) *Public Issues, Private Pain*, London Social Services Insight

Biehal, N. and Sainsbury, E. (1991) 'From values to rights in social work', *British Journal of Social Work*, 21, pp. 245-57

Boal, F. W. and Douglas, N. H. (1983) *Integration and Division: Geographical Perspectives on the Northern Ireland Problem*, London, Academic Press

Bolger, S., Corrigan, P., Docking, J. and Frost, N. (1981) *Towards Socialist Welfare Work*, London, Macmillan

Boyle, L. (1978) 'The Ulster Workers' Strike, May 1974', in Darby, J. and Williamson, A. (eds.), *Violence and the Social Services in Northern Ireland*, London, Heinemann

Brewer, J. (1991) 'The parallels between sectarianism and racism', in CCETSW, *One Step Towards Racial Justice: The Teaching of Antiracism in Diploma in Social Work Programmes*, London, CCETSW

British Association of Social Workers (1975) 'A code of ethics for social work', in Watson, A. (ed.) *A Code of Ethics for Social Work: The Second Stage*, London, Routledge and Kegan Paul

Campbell, J. (1986) *Violence: An Examination of the Role of Ideology in Various Interpretations of the Concept*, Unpublished Ph.D. Thesis, The Queen's University of Belfast

Central Council for Education and Training in Social Work (CCETSW) (1991) *Rules and Requirements for the Diploma in Social Work*, CCETSW Paper 30, 2nd edition, London, CCETSW

Chapman, T. and Pinkerton, J. (1987) 'Contradiction in community', *Probation Journal*, March, pp. 13-16

Clarke, C. and Asquith, S. (1985) *Social Work and Social Philosophy*, London, Routledge and Kegan Paul

Clarke, J. (1993) *A Crisis in Care*, London, Sage

Connolly, M. (1990) *Politics and Policy Making in Northern Ireland*, Hemel Hempstead, Philip Allan.

Corrigan, P. And Leonard, P. (1978) *Social Work Practice Under Capitalism*, London, Macmillan

Darby, J. and Williamson, A. (eds.) (1978) *Violence and the Social Services in Northern Ireland*, London, Heinemann

Davis, A. (1991) 'A structural approach to social work', in Lishman, J. (ed.) *Handbook of Theory for Practice Teachers*, London, Jessica Kingsley

Department of Health and Social Services (1969) *Children and Young Persons Act*, Belfast, HMSO

Department of Health and Social Services (1976) *Payment for Debts Act*, Belfast, HMSO

Ditch, J. (1983) 'Social policy in crisis'? The case of Northern Ireland', in Loney, M. *et al* (eds.) *Social Policy and Social Welfare*, Milton Keynes, Open University Press

Ditch, J. and Morrisey, M. (1992) 'Northern Ireland: review and prospects for social policy', *Social Policy and Administration*, 26, pp. 18-39

Dominelli, L. (1988) *Anti-Racist Social Work*, London, Macmillan

Eastern Health and Social Services Board (1992) *Raise the Issues*, Belfast, EHSSB

Evason, E. (1985) *On the Edge: A Study of Poverty and the Long Term Unemployed*, Derry, CPAG.

Gaffikin, F. and Morrisey, M. (1990) *Northern Ireland: The Thatcher Years*, London, Zed

Gallie, W. B. (1955) 'Essentially contested concepts', *Proceedings of the Aristotelian Society*, 56, pp. 167-98

Griffiths, H. (1978) 'Community reaction and voluntary involvement', in Darby, J. and Williamson, A. (eds.) *Violence and the Social Services in Northern Ireland*, London, Heinemann

Hanmer, J. and Statham, D. (1988) *Women and Social Work: Towards a Women-Centred Practice*, London, Macmillan

Harwin, J. (1993) 'Safe haven for dogma pedlars', *The Times Higher Educational Supplement*, 1 October 1993

Hugill, B. (1993) 'Terry's Mum fights the apartheid of Social Services', *The Observer*, 1 August 1993

Husband, C. (1992) 'A policy against racism', *The Psychologist*, September, pp. 414-15

John, P. (1993) *Local Government in Northern Ireland*, York, Joseph Rowntree Foundation

Jordan, B. (1990) *Social Work in an Unjust Society*, Hemel Hempstead, Harvester-Wheatsheaf

Kelly, G. (1979) 'Social work in courts in Northern Ireland', in Parker, H. (ed.) *Social Work and the Courts*, London, Edward Arnold

Leonard, P. (1976) 'Social control, class values and social work practice', *Social Work*, 28, p. 4

Logue, K. (1992) *Anti-Sectarianism and the Voluntary Sector and Community Sector*. Paper presented to Northern Ireland Community Relations Council Conference

O'Dowd, L., Rolston, B. and Tomlinson, M. (1980) *Northern Ireland: Between Civil Rights and Civil War*, London, CSE Books

Oliver, M. (ed.) (1991) *Social Work, Disabled People and Disabling Environments*, London, Jessica Kingsley

Phillips, M. (1993) 'Oppressive urge to stop oppression', *The Observer*, 1 August 1993

Pinker, R. (1993) 'A lethal kind of looniness', *The Times Higher Supplement*, 10 September 1993

Rojek, C., Peacock, G. and Collins, S. (1988) *Social Work and Received Ideas*, London, Routledge

Rolston, B. (1983) 'Reformism and sectarianism: the state of the union after civil rights', in Darby, J. (ed.) *Northern Ireland: The Background to the Conflict*, Belfast, Appletree

Rolston, B. and Smyth, M. (1982) 'The spaces between the cases: radical social work in Northern Ireland', in Bailey, R. and Lee, P. (eds.) *Theory and Practice in Social Work*, Oxford, Basil Blackwell

Simpkin, M. (1989) 'Radical social work: lessons for the 1990s', in Carter, P., Jeffs, T. and Smith, M. (eds.) *Yearbook of Social Work and Social Policy* 1, Milton Keynes, Open University Press

Smyth, M., Schlindwein, H. and Michael, G. (1993) *Aspects of Implementing Anti-Discriminatory Practice in Social Work Practice in Social Work Education in Northern Ireland: A Preliminary Study*, Derry, University of Ulster

Teague, P. (ed.) (1993) *The Northern Ireland Economy*, London, Lawrence and Wishart

Thompson, N. (1993) *Anti-Discriminatory Practice*, London, Macmillan

Wilson, D. and Wright, F. (1992) *Meeting Together: Trade Unionists, Intimidation and the Work Place*, Belfast, Counteract

Whyte, J. (1991) *Interpreting Northern Ireland*, Oxford, Clarendon

Acknowledgement
The authors wish to thank Dr John Pinkerton, Department of Social Work, The Queen's University of Belfast, for his helpful comments on an earlier draft of this paper.

PART 3

Directory and bibliographies

Chapter 7: Religious faith and communities: directory and select bibliographies for social workers

by Kaushika Amin

This book is not an A-Z guide about minority religions' philosophy, practices and customs. Nevertheless, in reality professionals do need such information to deal with specific circumstances. This chapter provides a useful reference guide for those who wish to be better informed on a particular religion or specific aspects of it.

The following guide to sources of information on religious faith and practice in ethnic minority communities is intended for use with other bibliographies and directories on ethnicity, race, and social work, notably *The Institute of Race Relations Guide to Resource Directory on 'race' and racism in social work*, 1993. The items listed in the bibliographies are a small selection of books, articles and pamphlets in each area which can be easily obtained from research libraries, make important contributions and provide background to faith and practice. As the focus is on religious faith and communities, the guide does not include general materials on ethnicity and racism except when they have a direct bearing on the subject.

Part 1 consists of a directory of national inter-faith organisations and religious organisations divided into faith and other sub-sections. It does not cover local inter-faith and religious organisations. Readers are advised to refer to *Religions in the UK: multi-faith directory* 1997 published by the Inter Faith Network and the Religious Resource and Research Centre, University of Derby for a comprehensive listing of religious organisations. Part 2 consists of a select bibliography on minority religions, while Part 3 is a bibliography on social work and religion also sub-divided. Most of the items mentioned have been selected because they place some emphasis on the religious background of minority communities or discuss more fully the implications of religion for the client group or for social work practice. Again these sections should be used with other sources of information on minority ethnic communities.

CONTENTS

Part 1: Inter-faith organisations
1.1	National inter-faith organisations	121
1.2	Christian churches and organisations	123
1.3	Buddhists	124
1.4	Hindu organisations	124
1.5	Muslim organisations	125
1.6	Sikh organisations	126

1.7 Centres and educational bodies   127
1.8 Academic centres offering courses   127
1.9 Race relations organisations   128

Part 2: Select bibliography on minority religions
2.1 General sources on minority religions   129
2.2 Diversity and inter-faith relations   132
2.3 Law   134
2.4 Church and race   135
2.5 Black Christians   138
2.6 Muslim communities   139
2.7 Sikhs   143
2.8 Buddhism   145
2.9 Hindu groups   145
2.10 Rastafarians   146
2.11 Women   148

Part 3: Bibliography on social work and religion
3.1 General sources on social work and religion   149
3.2 Children and families   152
3.3 Elderly people   154
3.4 Bereavement   155

PART 1: INTER-FAITH ORGANISATIONS

1.1 National inter-faith organisations

All Faiths for One Race, 27 Weston Road, Handsworth, Birmingham B19 1EH. Telephone: 0121 523 8076. AFFOR promotes inter-faith understanding and action to combat racism and intolerance. Publishes a newsletter and other occasional reports.

Churches Commission for Inter-faith Relations, Church House, Dean's Yard, Westminster, London SW1P 3NZ. Telephone: 0171 222 9011. Promotes good relations between the major Christian churches of Britain and Ireland and other faith communities. Publishes reports and provides information on inter-faith issues.

Council of Christians and Jews, 1 Dennington Park Road, West End Lane, London NW6 1AX. Telephone: 0171 794 8178/9. Aims to educate Christians and

Jews about each other's religious beliefs and to combat all forms of discrimination, especially antisemitism. Publishes a newsletter and journal, *Common Ground*, three times a year. The Council works through meetings and work with other organisations.

The Inner Cities Religious Council, Floor 4/K10, Eland House, Bressenden Place, London SW1E 5DU. Telephone: 0171 890 3703. The Council, formed in 1992, is located within the Department of Environment, Transport and Regions. Its aim is to enable the Government and the various faith communities to work together to address the problems faced by inner cities and deprived urban areas. The Council's activities cover policy development, information dissemination and promotion of practical activities. It acts as a catalyst in stimulating policy making and a "bridge" between the faith communities, government departments, local authorities, private sector, local communities and organisations. The Council publishes an informative newsletter *Faith Interaction*.

The Inter Faith Network for the United Kingdom, 5-7 Tavistock Place, London, WC1H 9SS. Telephone: 0171 388 0008. The network provides information and guidance on inter-faith matters to organisations and individuals. It produces excellent resources including a *Handbook of Affiliated Organisations*, which provides detailed information on the different faith organisations affiliated to the network, national and local inter-faith organisations and study centres and educational bodies working on inter-faith issues. Each entry includes the aims, details of membership and contact of each organisation. The network has published a range of reports and papers on inter-faith issues. Its most recent publication is *Religions in the* UK: *multi-faith directory* (1997) published jointly with the Religious Resource and Research Centre, University of Derby, which contains a comprehensive listing of religious and inter-faith organisations.

London Society of Jews and Christians, Liberal Jewish Synagogue, 28 St Johns Road, London NW8 7HA. Telephone: 0171 286 5181. Aims to increase understanding and co-operation between Jews and Christians. Organises meetings and gatherings.

Standing Conference of Jews, Christians and Muslims in Europe, Blackfriars, 36 Queens Drive, Glasgow, G42 8DD. Telephone: 0141 423 2971. Aims to encourage Jews, Christians and Muslims to work together to remove ignorance and combat prejudice. Organises meetings etc.

World Congress of Faiths, 28 Powis Gardens, London W11 1JG. Telephone: 0171 727 2607. Brings together committed followers of different religions to understand and appreciate each other's beliefs and values in a climate of mutual respect and trust. The WCF publishes a journal *World Faiths Encounter*, three times a year, free to members and £10 to non-members. It also organises lectures, seminars and retreats which are open to non-members as well as members and for which a small charge is made.

1.2 Christian churches and organisations

Afro-West Indian United Council of Churches, New Testament Church of God, Arcadian Gardens, Wood Green High Road, London, N22. Members of the Council are mainly Christian churches with predominantly Afro-Caribbean membership.

Churches Commission for Racial Justice, Council of Churches for Britain and Ireland, 35-41 Lower Marsh, London SE1 7RL. Telephone: 0171 620 4444. Promotes antiracism and action against inequality within churches and by churches within society. Publishes a bi-monthly journal *Church and Race*, which has reviews, news and commentary on race and churches issues in Britain.

Catholic Association of Racial Justice, St Vincent's Community Centre, Talma Road, Brixton, London SW2 1AS. Telephone: 0171 274 0024. National membership organisation of black and white Catholics working for racial justice in the church and wider society. Concerned with affirming the role of black Catholics in the church and developing a youth initiative on an ecumenical basis. Has an on-going educational publications programme.

Council of African and Afro-Caribbean Churches, 31 Norton House, Sidney Road, London SW9 OUJ. Telephone: 0171 274 5589. Membership is open to all churches and organisations regardless of denomination. Organises occasional conferences and disseminates information and publications.

Evangelical Christians for Racial Justice, 29 Trinity Road, Ashton, Birmingham B6 6AJ. Telephone: 0121 515 3885. ECRJ is an inter-denominational organisation devoted to fighting racism in the churches and society. It provides resources and training to support these aims by holding conferences, providing advice and making speakers available to churches and other organisations. It publishes a journal, *Racial Justice*, three times a year and other helpful publications.

General Synod's Board for Social Responsibility, Race and Community Relations Committee, Church House, Dean's Yard, Westminster, London SW1P 3NZ. Telephone: 0171 222 9011. The Committee has an advisory role within the Church of England on issues relating to racial justice. It liaises at local and national levels with organisations promoting racial equality.

Methodist Church, Committee for Racial Justice, Methodist Church, Room 405, 1 Central Buildings, Westminster, London SW1H 9NH. Telephone: 0171 222 8010. The committee aims to promote equal opportunities and racial justice within the Methodist Church and in society in general.

Simon of Cyrene Theological Trust, 2 St Anns Crescent, London SW18 2LR. Telephone: 0181 874 1353. Provides courses and arranges conferences to educate members of the mainstream and independent churches on black spirituality and religious experience.

1.3 Buddhists

London Buddhist Vihara, 5 Heathfield Gardens, Chiswick, London W4 4JU. Telephone: 0181 995 9493. Religious and cultural centre for Buddhists from all ethnic backgrounds. Publishes information and educational materials on Buddhism.

1.4 Hindu organisations

Brahma Kumaris World Spiritual University, Global Co-operation House, 65 Pound Lane, London NW10 2HH. Telephone: 0181 459 1400. Mainly involved in the dissemination of information and education on meditation, stress management and positive thinking. Runs courses and lectures. The organisation publishes a journal available on request/subscription.

The Hindu Centre, 39 Grafton Terrace, London NW5 4JA. Telephone: 0171 485 8200. Oldest Hindu centre in UK, the centre organises educational activities and religious occasions involving many different Hindu groups. It offers sitar and music classes, and Sanskrit courses.

The International Society for Krishna Consciousness (ISKCON), Bhaktivedanta Manor, Letchmore Heath, Nr. Watford, Herts, WD2 8EP. Telephone: 01923 857244. Essentially the centre of the Hare Krishna movement. The manor is a place of

pilgrimage, education and worship for many British Hindus. Publishes extensive publications and their monthly journal *Mahabharata Times*.

Jain Samaj Europe, 32 Oxford Street, Leicester LE1 5XU. Telephone: 0116 2543091. One of the largest religious and cultural centres for devotees of the Jain faith, the centre is a place of worship and social and community activities.

London Sevashram Sangha, 199a Devonport Road, Shepherds Bush, London W12 8PB. Telephone: 0181 749 2972. Used mainly by Hindus from Guyana and Trinidad, and by a minority from other countries including India and Mauritius. The centre is also used by non-Hindus for meditation and Yoga. It conducts a youth training project, language classes, certificate courses on Hinduism, training in meditation, and yoga. Members are happy to visit old and disabled people at home and hospital in London. Provides an advisory service and counselling in liaison with other similar organisations.

National Council for Hindu Temples, c/o Shree Sanatan mandir, Weymouth Street, off Catherine Street, Leicester; or Bhaktivedanta Manor, Nr. Watford, Herts WD2 8EP. Co-ordinates and represents Hindu temples in Britain. Organises festivals and events for Hindus of all age groups.

Swaminarayan Hindu Mission, Swami Complex, 54-62 Meadow Garth, Neasden, London NW10 8HD. Telephone: 0181 965 2651. A charitable organisation promoting Hindu religion and culture. Mainly used by Swaminarayans although members of other sects do use it. Runs an independent Hindu school.

Shri Venkateswara (Balaji) Temple of the UK, correspondence address is: 10 Slater Street, Great Bridge, Tipton, West Midlands, DY4 7EY. Telephone: 0121 557 7826. Used mainly by South Indian and Sri Lanka Hindus but also by Hindus from other parts of the world, this religious and cultural organisation aims to be non-sectarian and is involved in discussion with other faiths. It is in process of acquiring a property which would act as a centre for worship and community activities.

1.5 Muslim organisations

The Islamic Centre, Regent's Centre, Regent's Lodge, 146 Park Road, London NW8 7RG. Telephone: 0171 724 3363/7. Linked to the London Central Mosque, it provides information on the religious, educational and social needs of Muslim

communities. Publishes a monthly newsletter and *The Islamic Quarterly* journal.

Islamic Foundation, Markfield Dawah Centre, Ratby Lane, Markfield, Leicester LE67 9RN. Telephone: 0115 324 4944. The foundation is mainly involved in publishing and research. Its aim is to develop a better understanding of Islam among all people, Muslims and non-Muslims, in Britain. Runs courses for teachers, social workers and other professionals on issues concerning Muslims.

The Muslim Educational Trust, 130 Stroud Green Road, London N4 3RZ. Telephone: 0171 272 8502. Established in 1966, the MET is the oldest Muslim educational organisation dealing with the concerns of Muslim parents and children relating to schools and colleges. Publishes books and posters on Islam for use by young people and educationalists.

The Muslim Institute, 6 Endsleigh Street, London WC1H 0DS. Telephone: 0171 388 2581. Engaged in research and publication of reports concerning Muslims in Britain on a wide range of areas, the institute acts as think tank on Muslim issues forming a network of organisations such as the Muslim Parliament. Holds seminars and lectures, some of which have been published.

World Ahl Ul-Bayt (A.S) Islamic League (UK), 21 Lavington Drive, Longleven, Gloucester GL2 0HW. Telephone: 01452 423 578. Membership is open to Shia organisations and individuals. Aims to create a better understanding between Shia and other Muslim and non-Muslim communities. Holds conferences and seminars and publishes occasional papers.

World Islamic Mission (UK), 17 Burston Drive, Park Street, St Alban's, Hertfordshire. Telephone: 01727 72511. Membership is open to Muslims. Holds meetings and publishes books on Islam.

1.6 Sikh organisations

Kalsa College, London, 76 Gayton Road, Harrow, Middlesex HA1 2LS. Telephone: 0181 428 4052. Provides training and workshops on Sikh culture and religion. Publishes books on Sikhism for non-Sikhs and people from other cultures.

The Sikh Cultural Society of Great Britain, 88 Mollison Way, Edgware, Middlesex HA8 5QW. Telephone: 0181 952 1215. Provides general information

and literature on Sikhism free of charge. An educational centre for culture and religion, it publishes a journal, *The Sikh Courier*, four times a year.

Sikh Missionary Society, 10 Featherstone Road, Southall, Middlesex UB2 5AA. Telephone: 0181 574 1902. A charitable organisation which arranges lectures, celebrates religious festivals of the Sikh faith and publishes literature on various aspects of Sikhism.

1.7 Centres and educational bodies

Bharatiya Vidya Bhavan, Institute of Indian Culture, 4A Castletown Road, London W14 9HQ. Telephone: 0171 381 3086. A secular and non-political educational organisation, the institute provides classes in the various Indian languages, performing arts, and yoga and holds concerts, dance recitals. There is a bookshop on music, languages, food education, archaeology and philosophy and various aspects of Indian culture. Has a newsletter available to members – details from the centre.

Centre for the Study of Islam and Christian-Muslim Relations, Selly Oak Colleges, 996 Bristol Road, Birmingham B29 6LQ. Telephone: 0121 472 4231. The centre is a place of meeting between Christians and Muslims who wish to grow in understanding of the religious traditions of Islam and Christianity. It offers full or part-time studies as part of a general studies programme, a diploma in Islam and a research programme on Islam in Europe. It publishes regular research reports on Islam in Britain and Europe.

Multi-faith Centre, Harborne Hall, Old Church Road, Harborne, Birmingham B17 0BD. Telephone: 0121 427 1044. The directors and teaching staff of the multi-faith centre are members of the Hindu, Muslim, Sikh, Buddhist, Jewish and Christian traditions. It has a permanent team of multi-faith, multicultural educators and resource personnel from their communities. The team design and arrange programmes to meet the specific needs of teachers, health and social workers and other professionals.

1.8 Academic centres offering courses

Religious Resource and Research Centre, University of Derby, Mickleover, Derby DE3 5GX. Telephone: 01332 47181. The centre is a joint initiative of the College

and the Anglican Dioceses of Derby. It maintains a computer database on local religious communities and organisations and is happy to provide information in response to enquiries. It monitors religious issues and wider public and academic debates concerned with human value. A programme of lectures, seminars and discussions open to the public is provided. It is jointly working with the Inter Faith Network to produce a multi-faith directory of religious life and organisations in the UK. Introductory and academic courses are also offered by many universities and institutions of further education. These include:

Religious Resource and Research Centre, University of Derby, Mickleover, Derby DE3 5GX. Telephone: 01332 47181.

Community Relations Project, Department of Theology and Religious Studies, University of Leeds.

Religious Studies Department, University of Newcastle upon Tyne NE1 7RU.

Religious Education Project, University of Warwick, Coventry CV4 7AL. Telephone: 01203 523523.

Edinburgh University, Divinity and Religious Studies, New College, Mouth Place, Edinburgh EHl 21X. Telephone: 0131 225 8400.

Roehampton Institute, Theology and Religious Studies, Southlands College, 65 Parkside, Wimbledon, London SW19 SNN. Telephone: 0181 392 3000.

School of Oriental and African Studies, Religious Studies Department, Thornhaugh Street, Russell Square, London WC1H OXG. Telephone: 0171 637 2388.

1.9 Race relations organisations

Commission for Racial Equality, 10-12 Allington St, London SW1E 5EH. Telephone: 0171 828 7022. Set up under the Race Relations Act 1976, the Commission works towards the elimination of discrimination and promotes good race relations. A range of reports amd leaflets is published and a journal, *New Community*, comes out three/four times a year. Also publishes a list of community relations councils which can be a helpful source of information at a local level. Many local race equality councils publish newsletters and reports of research on local issues.

Centre for Research in Ethnic Relations, University of Warwick, Arts Building, University of Warwick, Coventry CV4 7AL. Telephone: 01203 24011. A principal centre for academic research on race relations issues in Britain, many of its publications are increasingly concerned with religious identity and diversity. It publishes a series of research papers, as well as bibliographies.

Institute of Race Relations, 2-6 Leeke Street, Kings Cross Road, London WC1X 9HX. Telephone: 0171 837 0041. Established in 1958 to promote the study of race relations, the institute has a library on race and racism. Publishes a quarterly journal, *Race and Class*, and other publications on policing, feminism and racism in Europe and Britain. It has also published books on community care and a bibliography on race and social work.

The Race Relations Research Unit, 1 Mannville Terrace, Bradford, West Yorkshire BD7 1BA. Telephone: 01274 753468. The unit is a joint initiative for academic collaboration between the University of Bradford and Bradford & Ilkley College. It provides a forum for advancing policy related race relations, disseminates current research, and publishes occasional books and papers.

Runnymede Trust, 133 Aldersgate Street, London EC1A 4JA. Telephone: 0171 600 9666. The trust collects and disseminates information and promotes public education in race relations and immigration. It publishes a range of books and reports and *The Runnymede Bulletin* monthly.

Scottish Ethnic Minorities Research Unit, Glasgow College of Technology, Cowcaddens Road, Glasgow G4 OBA. Telephone: 0141 332 7090, or Edinburgh College of Art/Heriot University Place, Edinburgh EH3 9DF. Telephone: 0131 229 9311. The unit carries out independent research on ethnic minorities in Scotland, acts as resource centre for research and arranges conferences, seminars and teaching programmes. Publishes reports on issues such as racial violence and social services.

PART 2: SELECT BIBLIOGRAPHY ON MINORITY RELIGIONS

2.1 General sources on minority religions

Ballard, R. (ed.) (1994) *Desh Pardesh: the South Asian presence in Britain* Hurst & Company, 296pp., £9.95. This collection of articles written by respected academics shows how communities maintain family links and generate community solidarity on the basis of common religious ties and family loyalties.

Barley, L. M. *et al.* (1987) *Religion: Reviews of United Kingdom Statistical Sources* Volume 20, The Royal Statistical Society, Economic and Social Research Council and Pergamon Press 621pp. A reference guide to sources of statistical material of all

kinds, both official and unofficial. Sections on Christian sources, Judaism, and other religions.

Beckerlegge, G. (1991) '"Strong", cultures and distinctive religions: the influence of imperialism upon British communities of South Asian origin' in *New Community*, Volume 17, no 2, January. This interesting article challenges the contrast – based on distinctive religion and adherence to culture – often drawn between "weak" Afro-Caribbean and "strong" South Asian culture. It examines the reasons for the prominent role that religion plays in the creation of formal associations of South Asian groups. The article concludes that the contrast is unhelpful not only because of its negative evaluation of Caribbean culture but also because of its uncritical view of the strengths of Asian culture.

Brierley, P. and Longley, D. (1991) UK *Christian Handbook* 1992/93 *Edition*. An important source of information on religious observance and affiliation based on information from organisations within the communities themselves.

Collins, D., Tank, M. and Basith, A. (1993) *Concise Guide to Customs of Minority Ethnic Religions* Arena. Condenses into a handy pocket-sized book a variety of useful basic information about Judaism, Hinduism, Islam, Sikhism, Vietnamese Buddhism and ancestor-worship, Chinese Buddhism, Confucianism and Taoism, and Rastafarianism.

Community Relations Council (1976) *Between Two Cultures: a study of relationships in the Asian Community in Britain* 73pp. An examination of the cultural contrast experienced by young Asians between two cultures, one in the home and the other taught at school. The study focuses on the sources and types of stresses, tensions and conflicts this contrast produces.

The Guardian (undated) *The Faiths: Education Guardian Religions Source Book* 23pp. A collection of articles on world faiths which featured in the pages of the Guardian's Tuesday educational supplement. Sections on Anglicanism, Catholicism, Churches, Islam, Judaism, Hinduism, Sikhism, Buddhism and Humanism.

Hinnells, I. (ed.) (1991) *A Handbook of Living Religions* Penguin Books, 528 pp. Scholarly articles on major religions by experts in their fields – Judaism, Christianity, Islam, Zoroastrianism, Hinduism, Sikhism, Jainism, Buddhism, Chinese religions, Japanese religion and new religious movements. Each article

provides descriptions, not only of official teaching, but also of popular practices, sources and interpretation, tradition and history.

Holroyde, P. (1970) *East comes West: a background to some Asian faiths* Community Relations Council 88pp. An introductory book on the three major religions practised by people of South Asian origin. Describes general philosophy, key concepts and festivals.

Hutnik, N. (1985) 'Aspects of identity in a multi-ethnic society' in *New Community* Volume XII, No 2, Summer, pp.298-309. Based on research carried out in 1983, this article explores the social identity components of 105 young people from three ethnic groups in Britain, namely South Asian, Afro-Caribbean, and English. Religion was the second major market for the South Asian group, while for the Afro-Caribbean young people, the race or colour variable was extremely significant. The article confirms that minority group adolescents use nationality, religious and racial distinctions in the process of self-definition.

Jeffery, P. (1976) *Migrants and Refugees: Muslim and Christian Pakistani families in Bristol* Cambridge University Press 221pp. This early study looks at the experiences of a small group of Muslim and Christian Pakistani families in Britain. It concentrates on family life, leisure patterns and religious adherence. The author suggests that their perception and attachment to Britain may be explained by their different positions in Pakistan and their aspirations.

Johnson, M. R. D. (1985) '"Race", religion and ethnicity: religious observance in the West Midlands' in *Ethnic and Racial Studies* Volume 8, no 3, July, pp. 426-437. Part of an ERSC survey which collected data on religious affiliation and observance along with other information on social characteristics in the West Midlands.

Knott, K. (1986) *Religion and Identity, and the study of Ethnic Minority Religions in Britain* Community Religions Project, University of Leeds, 16pp. This paper suggests that religion is an important factor in the formation of ethnic identity. It describes the different perspectives from which the complex relations between identity, ethnicity and religion have been examined. The author argues that religion is made dynamic and changing through factors such as migration and settlement.

Modood, T. (1992) *Not easy being British: colour, culture and citizenship* Runnymede Trust and Trentham Books 93pp. In a collection of articles, reviews and papers,

the author records the seeming emergence of a Muslim identity. He examines current patterns of employment and disadvantage, religion and identity, and reactions to the Salmon Rushdie affair and calls for a radical re-thinking of our understanding of race relations and equal opportunities.

Modood, T., Beishon, S. and Virdee, S. (1994) *Changing Ethnic Identities* Policy Studies Institute 125pp. The first comparative study of African, Caribbean and South Asian groups on what their ethnic backgrounds means to them. It examines the basis of ethnic identity in family life, community languages, religion, marriage choices and in experiences of racial exclusion. The authors conclude that we need a new view of Britishness and the varieties and forms that it can take.

Modood, T., Berthoud, R., Lakey, J., Nazroo, J., Smith, P., Virdee, S., Beishon, S. (1997) *Ethnic Minorities in Britain: diversity and disadvantage*, Policy Studies Institute 416 pp. This is the fourth national survey of ethnic minorities in Britain from the PSI, a major report considering life experience of minority ethnic groups in several sectors. The survey highlighted the importance of religion in self-description and identity and provides a focus on culture and identity.

Parrinder, G. (1964) *The World's Living Religions* Pan, 203pp. This book gives a short and impartial account of the main religions in the modern world. Each religion is approached through the worship of its followers, followed by a brief history, a summary of its principal teachings and estimates of movements of reform and revival. Like other books by Geoffery Parrinder, it is admirably unbiased and thorough.

Watson, J. L. (1977) *Between Two Cultures: migrants and minorities in Britain* Basil Blackwell, 338pp. The work of 12 anthropologists whose focus on ethnic minorities is from both ends of the migration chain – in the migrants' country of origin and in Britain. The chapters on Sikhs, Pakistanis and Jamaicans are particularly interesting.

2.2 Diversity and inter-faith relations

Brown, S. (1994) *The Nearest in Affection: Towards a Christian Understanding of Islam* World Council of Churches 124pp. Sets out to examine questions based on the inter-faith relationship between Christians and Muslims by giving an overview of

what Muslims believe and where their beliefs and practices reveal points of contact with and divergence from Christianity.

Commission for Racial Equality and the Runnymede Trust (1990) *Britain: a Plural Society: report of a seminar* CRE Discussion Paper 3, 78pp. Four papers on the difficulties of reconciling social cohesion and national integration with proper respect for cultural diversity and autonomy. Interesting papers by distinguished writers on the theoretical, legal and practical consideration of pluralism.

D'Costa, G. (1986) *Theology and Religious Pluralism: the challenge of other religions* Basil Blackwell 155pp. Examines the relationship between Christianity and other religions. Drawing from his own and other people's experience of dialogue with other faiths, the author discusses how Christianity can come to terms with a world of religious pluralism without either closing its eyes to the challenges posed by other faiths or compromising its own central beliefs.

D'Costa, G. (ed.) (1990) *Christian Uniqueness Reconsidered: the myth of a pluralistic theology of religions* Orbis. In response to an increasing acceptance of a pluralist view in the theology of religions, contributors in the book challenge the assumption that the Christian faith is just one among many on issues of salvation and truth.

Hooker, R. and Sargant, I. (eds.) (undated) *Belonging to Britain: Christian perspectives on religion and identity in a plural society* The Committee for Relations with other Faiths, 172pp. In this interesting volume various members of the Committee for Relations with Other Faiths explore the meaning of nationality and Christian identity from biblical, historical, feminist and black perspectives. Of particular interest are chapter 1: 'What is a nation? The biblical understanding and the Christian interpretation' by Kenneth Cracknell; chapter 2: 'Victorian values? Some antecedents of a religiously plural society' by Peter Bishop; chapter 3: 'Land of hope and glory' by Sybil Phoenix; chapter 8: 'Integrity and affirmation: inclusivist approach to national identity' by Brenda Watson and chapter 9: 'Some reflections on the essays' by Gavin D'Costa.

Inter Faith Network (1991) *Statement on Inter-Religious Relations in Britain* 6pp.

Inter Faith Network (1991) *Handbook of Affiliated Organisations*. An excellent resource for organisations interested in religious dialogue and inter-faith contact.

All the entries are detailed using a standardised format under the headings of membership, aims, publications etc. An important resource for anyone concerned with religious diversity.

Marshall. E. (ed.). (1997) *Business Ethics: The Religious Dimension*, Working Paper No. 9705, The Management Centre, University of Bradford. This interesting report comprises of conference papers which considers the ethical basis of management with Christian, Muslim, and Buddhist approaches to business ethics.

Moore, P. (1992) *World Religions and the Problems of Christian Universalism* World Faiths Encounter, No 3, November, 1322pp. Considers some of the difficulties that Christianity as a religion of universal salvation raises for the theology of religions and for inter-faith dialogue.

Weller, P. (ed.) (1997) *Religions in the* UK: *a multi-faith directory* The University of Derby in association with The Inter Faith Network for the United Kingdom. Provides detailed coverage of the extraordinary diversity of religious belief and practice in the UK, dealing with the Baha'i, Buddhist, Christian, Hindu, Jain, Jewish, Muslim, Sikh and Zoroastrian communities, as well as with inter-faith activity, organisations and groups.

2.3 Law

Coliver, S. (ed.) (1992) *Striking a Balance: hate speech, freedom of expression and non-discrimination* Article 19, London and Human Rights Centre, University of Essex, 417pp. One of 27 articles examining the laws which regulate hate speech in 14 countries. Articles on British laws explain their limitations with regard to insult and prejudice on religious grounds.

Commission for Racial Equality (1990) *Free Speech: report of a seminar* 118pp. Collection of papers presented at a seminar which deal with the nature and limits of free speech in a culturally and religiously diverse society.

Commission for Racial Equality and the Inter Faith Network (1990) *Law, Blasphemy and the Multi-Faith Society* 99pp. Papers from a seminar organised by the CRE and the Inter Faith Network on the law of blasphemy and the case for its abolition, extension or replacement with new legal provisions.

Commission for Racial Equality and the Inter Faith Network (1990) *Law, Respect for Religious Identity and the Multi-Faith Society* 56pp. Explores in more detail a variety of legal options to protect religious sensibilities, and the case for and against the use of law at all in this field.

Preston-Shoot, M. (1998) *Acting Fairly: working within the law to promote equal opportunities in education and training* CCETSW 100pp. The book is a practical guide to understanding equal opportunities legislation (race, gender, disability, Welsh language, fair employment in Northern Ireland) and its application to social work practice. It contains useful examples and questions to make sense of the equal opportunities legislation. Its UK-wide application and specific focus to social work makes this a very useful guide to acting fairly.

Sebastian, P. (1990) *Asian Traditions and English Law* The Runnymede Trust with Trentham Books 154pp. A handbook which comprehensively covers the relationship between Asian cultures and the English legal system. Topics include marriage, divorce, parents and children and religious worship and observance. Each chapter covers cultural customs and religious practices and details of English law on each subject. Free from legal jargon. Useful for anyone who has to give advice and assistance.

2.4 Church and race

Adler, E. (1974) *A Small Beginning: an assessment of the first five years of the Programme to Combat Racism* World Council of Churches 120pp.

British Council of Churches (1988) *Rainbow Gospel: report of a churches conference on 'Challenging Racism in Britain',* 58pp. A collection of papers presented at a conference in November 1987 on racism in Britain and abroad.

Board of Mission and Unity of the Church of England (1984) *Towards the Theology of Inter-Faith Dialogue* CIO Publishing 41pp. Considers the theological aspects and implications of inter-faith dialogue in the changed context for British Christians. Refers to the main biblical pointers.

Board for Social Responsibility (1986) *Anglicans and Racism: the Balshall Heath consultation 1986* 50pp. Addresses, reports and recommendations made to the second consultation on the Church of England and Racism, which met at

Balshall Heath in Birmingham in 1986. The four addresses are: (1) 'Towards a Black Theology of liberation' by Sandra Wilson; (2) 'Response' by Rowan Williams; (3) 'Combating racism in the Church of England' by Kenneth Leech, and (4) 'A black Anglican perspective' by Barney Pityana.

Catholic Truth Society: (1989) *The Church and Racism* 45pp. Examines the development of racist ideologies and behaviour through history up to today's Britain. Calls for a Christian response to racial injustice.

Foward, M. (ed.) (1989) *God of All Faith: discerning God's presence in a multi-faith society* Methodist Church Home Mission Division. Contributions from members of the Methodist church on inter-faith issues. Includes questions and suggestions for group discussions.

The General Synod of the Church of England (1991) *Seeds of Hope: report of a survey on instruments for combating racism in the dioceses of the Church of England* by the Committee on Black Anglicans Concerns 35pp. Based on a survey of 12 dioceses, this report gives examples of good practice and the work being done to combat racism in dioceses. It recommends and encourages the Church of England at all levels to think theologically about racial justice issues and to place them on a higher level of priority.

General Synod Board of Mission (1992) *Multi-Faith Worship?* Church House Publishing. A historical and theological exploration of multi-faith worship in England. The booklet offers principles and suggestions to help individuals respond thoughtfully to multi-faith services and meetings. Includes a useful bibliography on inter-faith dialogue.

Cardinal Hume's Advisory Group on the Catholic Church's Commitment to the Black Community (undated) *With You in Spirit?* 97pp. A report on racism within the institutional structures of the Catholic Church and in the attitudes and practices of individual white Catholics.

Hick, J. (1979) *Christianity and Race in Britain Today* Affor 15pp. Using clear and unemotional facts on immigration and ethnic minority communities, the author suggests how Christians and the churches should respond to issues surrounding racial justice and equality.

Hick, I. and Knitter, P. (eds.) (1987) *The Myth of Christian Uniqueness: towards a pluralistic theology of religions* Orbis. Describes the many routes through which different faiths can approach the Truth.

Holden, B. and Rolls, E. (1992) *Christian Community and Cultural Diversity* National Centre for Christian Communities and Networks 43pp. Examines the ways in which Christian groups are seeking to relate to those of other races and faiths within British society. A useful resources section is included.

Holden, T. (1979) *From Race to Politics* AFFOR 16pp. A Christian perspective on racism and injustice, describing the main issues on race and pluralism in Britain.

Hope, S. (1992) *Liberty to the Captives (Christianity, racism and the law in the* UK) The Iona Community Working Group on Inter-faith and racism, 32pp. Argues with conviction and passion for the strengthening of race relations legislation.

Horton, J. and Crabtree, H. (1992) *Toleration and Integrity in a Multi-Faith Society* Department of Politics, University of York 79pp. Papers presented at a conference sponsored by the Inter Faith Network and the Morrell Studies in Toleration at the University of York. Includes papers from representatives of different faith communities on their religious tradition's resources and limitations for tolerating the other faith communities.

Kendall, E. R. (1982) *Christianity and Race* Community and Race Relations Unit, British Council of Churches 55pp. An analysis of the historical and modern relations of the churches and race. Includes sections on the nature of racism and the European dimension.

Leech, K. (1982) *Religion and the rise of racism* The Tawney memorial lectures, Christian Socialist Movement 15pp. Describes the impact of the Christian socialist R. H. Tawney on our understanding of the relationship between racism and religion.

Leech, K. (1986) *The Fields of Charity and Sin: Reflections on combating racism in the Church of England*, Race Pluralism and Community Group, Board for Social Responsibility 14pp. Based on his experience as a race relations field officer with the Church of England, the author reflects on issues of racial justice and equality in the Church's own structures.

Leech, K. (1988) *Struggle in Babylon: racism in the cities and churches of Britain* Sheldon Press 253pp. An important book about race, racism and the response of churches in inner city areas. Extracting from his own personal experiences and political climates, Kenneth Leech offers a powerful analysis of how class, race and the culture of affluence has divided British cities. There are chapters on theology, government practice, the church and politics.

Leech, K. (1992) *The Eye of the Storm: spiritual resources for the pursuit of justice* Darton, Longman and Todd 288pp. A major book examining the need for spiritual resources which can support and sustain the search for a just society. The book was a winner of the 1993 Harper Collins Religious Book Award.

2.5 Black Christians

Charman, P. (undated) *Reflections: black and white Christians in the City* Zebra Project 64pp. Speaking from personal experience, the author describes the sentiments, attitudes and behaviour of black and white Christians.

Grant, P. and Patel, R. (eds.) (1990) *A Time to Speak: perspectives of black Christians in Britain* CRRU/ECRJ 93pp. Written from the perspective of Afro-Caribbean and Asian Christians this unique collection of articles examines the ethnic minority experience in Britain. Includes articles on black theology, black women, issues for the black minister and racism. Highly recommended.

Hill, C. (1963) *West Indian Migrants and the London Churches* Oxford University Press 89pp. Early study of the participation of Afro-Caribbean immigrants in the religious life of London. Also includes information on religious and cultural practices.

Howard, V. (1987) *A report on Afro-Caribbean Christianity in Britain* Community Religions Project, University of Leeds 55pp. Contains useful information on the historical and social background of Afro-Caribbean Christians, and the contribution of racism and settlement experiences to the growth of black-led churches and adherence to historic churches.

Pryce, K. (1979) *Endless Pressure* Penguin Books 297pp. Based on personal experience and interviews with early West Indian immigrants, this unique study charts the stresses, pressures and discrimination faced by immigrants in Bristol. Includes sections on identity and involvement in black churches.

Watson, H. (1985) A *Tree God Planted: black people in Methodism* Ethnic minorities in Methodism Working Party 73pp. The historical and current participation of black people in the Methodist Church. Gives useful statistical background on black Methodists, involvement in church life and the relationship to wider society. Very readable.

Wilkinson, J., Wilkinson, R. and Evans, J. E. (1985) *Inheritors Together: black people in the church of England* Race, Pluralism and Community Group, Board for Social Responsibility 72pp. This collection of articles deals with the experiences and issues facing black Anglicans in Britain.

2.6 Muslim communities

Abdulla, R. (1992) *Where is the Muslim in me?* World Faiths Encounter, No. 3, November. A beautifully written examination of the complexity of the writer's own identity. Very readable and highly recommended.

Abedin, S. Z. and Ziauddin, S. (eds.) (1995) *Muslim minorities in the West* Grey Seal Books, 212pp. Fourteen scholars examine the problems of cultural change facing minority Muslim communities in the west. While struggling with racism and issues of identity, Muslim migrants want the west to know that they have come not only to live here, but to teach, learn, and live in peace and understanding with all their neighbours.

Anwar, M. (1979) *The Myth of Return: Pakistanis in Britain* Heinemann Educational, 278pp. A study of the Pakistani community and the social and kinship networks that exist within it. Helpful as a general reader covering culture, religion, employment patterns and political organisation.

Anwar, M. (1993) *Muslims in Britain: 1991 Census and Other Statistical Sources* CISC Paper No. 9, Centre for the Study of Islam and Christian-Muslim Relations, Selly Oak Colleges, Birmingham B29 6LQ. Uses the 1991 Census and other statistical sources to estimate the total UK Muslim population (1.5 million in 1993, according to Anwar) and to chart demographic, employment and housing trends.

Barton, S. W. (1986) *The Bengali Muslims of Bradford* Community Religions Project, Department of Theology and Religious Studies, University of Leeds, 244pp. A descriptive account of the observance of Islam within the Bengali Muslim

community in Bradford. Includes discussion on the process of migration, population estimates and forms of leadership exercised within the community.

McDermott, Y. M. and Ahsan, M. M. (1980) *The Muslim Guide: for teachers, employers, community and social administrators in Britain* The Islamic Foundation, 104pp. Outlines the religion and culture of Islam, providing a clear view on a variety of issues such as belief and conduct, attitudes to dress and food, education, and birth and death. A readable and comprehensive account of Islamic religion and practices.

El-Solh, C. F. (1991) 'Somalis in London's East End: a community striving for recognition' in *New Community* Volume 17, No 4, July. pp. 539-553. Traces the pattern of the Somali community's settlement in the Tower Hamlets area of London's East End. Analyses some of the obstacles which stand in the way of Somalis' quest for recognition.

El-Solh, C.F. (1993) '"Be True to your Culture": gender tensions among Somali Muslims in Britain' in *Immigrants & Minorities* Volume 12, No. 1, March, pp. 21-46. Explores the manner in which Somali Muslim women in London's East End negotiate their gender, ethnic and religious identities along paths which are meaningful to their life as migrants and refugees in Britain. The article also offers a glimpse of the settlement history and experiences of Somalis in Britain as well as reflections on their identities as Muslims.

Ellis, J. (1991) *A study of Muslim communities in Coventry* Centre for Research in Ethnic Relations, 145pp. Examines relations between identifiable groups within the Muslim community and between the various groups and the City Council. The report examines Coventry City Council's employment and service policies and practices and finds them failing Muslim communities.

Hussain, A. (1992) *Beyond Islamic Fundamentalism: the sociology of faith and action* Volcano Press, 163pp. A textbook on Islamic sociology and methodology examining major themes in the Muslim world.

IQRA Trust (1991) *Islam in Britain, Information for Parliament* 4pp. A report of a survey of knowledge of Islam in the UK. Outlines some general and educational issues concerning British Muslims.

IQRA (undated) *Research on Public Attitudes to Islam* Research report No. 1. Detailed report on a survey by MORI of the level of knowledge, experience and understanding of Islam among the general public.

Joly, D. (1995) *Britain's Crescent: making a place for Muslims in British society* Avebury, 197pp. The visibility of Muslims coupled with expressions of social and political concerns has put them in the public spotlight above other ethnic minority groups. Often this has led to increased prejudice against them. This book discusses the central issues pertaining to Muslim communities today. It examines the role of community organisations, the views of Muslim parents, the impact of Islam as it entered the public sphere and considers some of the responses made by public sector agencies.

Joly, D. and Nielsen, J. (1985) *Muslims in Britain: an annotated bibliography* 1960-1984 Centre for Research in Ethnic Relations, 35pp. Brings together references to work on different Muslim communities in Britain.

Lewis, P. (1994) *Islamic Britain: Religion, Politics and Identity Among British Muslims: Bradford in the 1990s* I. B. Tauris, 250pp. In this book, Bradford serves as a microcosm to study the achievements and predicaments faced by Muslims everywhere who have abandoned the "myth of return" that sustained the pioneer migrants and who are struggling to develop a British Muslim identity.

Nielsen, J. S. (undated) *Exploring Claims of Muslim Populations in Matters of Family Law* Paper No. 10, Centre for the Study of Islam and Christian-Muslim Relations, Selly Oak Colleges, Birmingham B29 6LQ. Explores the parameters constraining European implementation of Islamic law on marriage, divorce, inheritance and custody of children.

Nielsen, J. S. (1984) *Muslim Immigration and Settlement* Centre for the Study of Islam and Christian-Muslim Relations, 20pp. Discusses the immigration and settlement of Muslim communities across Britain.

Nielsen, J. S. (1987) 'Muslims in Britain: searching for an identity?' in *New Community*, Volume 13, No. 3, Spring, pp. 384-394. Argues that it is now possible to speak of the Muslim community in Britain even though factors of division such as ethnicity and socio-economic background continues to exist. Includes statistical and historical data on Muslims in Britain.

Peach, C. (1990) 'The Muslim Population of Great Britain' in *Ethnic and Racial Studies* Volume 13, No. 3 July pp. 414-419. Authoritative estimates of various Muslim communities in Britain including, Turkish Cypriot, Arab, and other smaller communities.

Rath, J., Groenendijik, K. and Penninx, R (1991) 'The recognition and institutionalisation of Islam in Belgium, Great Britain and the Netherlands' in *New Community* Volume 18, No. 1, October, pp. 101-114. Argues that historically specific laws and regulation with regard to different religious groups in Britain, Belgium and the Netherlands provoke different political reactions to the presence of Muslims. These laws also affect the representation of Muslims in these different countries.

Raza, M. S. (1991) *Islam in Britain: past, present and the future* Volcano Press, 120pp. Written by the director of the Islamic centre in Leicester, this book provides an account of Muslims in Britain. Includes chapters on class structure, political participation, Muslim women and freedom and the place of Islam in British society.

Robinson, F. (1988) *Varieties of South Asian Islam* Research paper in ethnic relations No. 8, Centre for Research in Ethnic Relations, 27pp. A well written examination of the origins of Islamic movements and groups of South Asian origin in Britain. It explores the relationships between different groups and their likely attitude to state and society in the western world. Useful as background.

Sajid, A. (1992) *Muslim Tradition and Liberal Values* World Faiths Encounter No. 2, July. A personal exploration by the director of the Briton Islamic Centre of the views of traditionalists and liberals on the history and experience of Muslim societies.

Samad, Y. (1992) 'Book burning and race relations: political mobilisation of Bradford Muslims' in *New Community* Volume 18, No. 4, July, pp. 507-519. Considers why Muslim identity has become politicised at this point in time and what made Bradford the centre of the storm against *The Satanic Verses*.

Sarwar, G. (1982) *Islam: beliefs and teachings* The Muslim Educational Trust, 236pp. The director of the Muslim Educational Trust describes the key aspects of Islam. Written largely for young people, the book provides clear and concise outlines of Islamic law, family life, marriage, status and the political and economic system of Islam.

Scantlebury, E. (1995) 'Muslims in Manchester: the depiction of a religious community' in *New Community* Volume 21, No. 3, pp. 425-435. Describes the emergence of a British Muslim identity that is effectively crossing racial and ethnic barriers in some circumstances within a localised setting.

Shaw, A. (1988) A *Pakistani Community in Britain* Basil Blackwell, 187pp. Based on a study of Pakistani families in Oxford, this book emphasises that the community's religious and cultural practices, far from disappearing, are adapting to life in Britain. The book looks at households and family relationships, Muslim castes and marriages, religious issues such as the influence of mosques and Islamic values, and finally at issues concerning the second generation.

Vertovec, S. (1993) *Annotated Bibliography of Academic Publications regarding Islam and Muslims in the United Kingdom*, 1985-1992, Centre for Research in Ethnic Relations, University of Warwick, No. 11 in the Bibliography series. A useful guide to books, articles and reports within the subject area.

Wahhab, I. (1989) *Muslims in Britain: profile of a community* The Runnymede Trust A descriptive account of the Muslim presence in Britain. Covers settlement patterns, population estimates, role of mosques, and some important concerns such as burial and education.

Werbner, P. (1990) *The Migration Process: capital, gifts and offerings among British Pakistanis* Berg Publishers, 391pp. This anthropological study of British Pakistanis in Manchester examines the cultural dimensions of their entrepreneurship, trading networks and the involvement of families and other kin.

Wilkinson, I. (1988) *Muslim Beliefs and Practices in a non-Muslim Country: a study of Rochdale* Centre for the Study of Islam and Christian-Muslim Relations, 28pp. Based on interviews with 20 Muslim men and women and information from representatives of some mosques in Rochdale, this study discusses some of the issues facing Muslims in Britain.

2.7 Sikhs

Arora, R. (1986) *Sikhism* Religions of the World series, Wayland Publishers. Provides a useful introduction to the key aspects of Sikhism written by an educationist from a Sikh background.

Bhachu, P. (1984) 'East African Sikhs in Britain: Experienced settlers with traditionalistic values' in *Immigrants and Minorities* Volume 3, No. 3, November, pp. 276-296. Deals with East African Sikhs whose pattern of migration is different from migrants from the Sub-continent and Pakistan.

Dhanjal, B. (1987) *Sikhism* B.T. Batford, 72pp. A dictionary of the philosophical and religious beliefs of Sikhism. Also describes Punjabi cultural practices. Illustrated with photographs and maps. Useful as background information.

James, A. G. (1974) *Sikh Children in Britain* Oxford University Press, 117pp. An interpretative and sensitive account of Sikhs living in Britain, this book examines the extent to which social and religious traditions of the Sikh community are being maintained in Sikh households in the UK, through discussions of family life, the upbringing of children, religious observance and of adolescence. The author argues that Sikh children are developing an awareness of their particular identity through racism and through tension and change in their community life.

Kalsi, S. S. (1992) *The Evolution of a Sikh Community in Britain* Department of Theology and Religious Studies, University of Leeds, 226pp. Through informal interviews and personal observation, this author discusses the dynamics of caste and kinship among the Sikh community in Leeds. He draws attention to the overlapping boundaries between religious and caste practices which have resulted in the development of a definite Sikh identity but also a particular identity such as Ramgarhia Sikh or iat Sikh, etc.

McCormack, M. K. (1988) *An Introduction to Sikh Belief* The Sikh Cultural Society of Great Britain, 16pp. Gives a brief outline of Sikh beliefs and practices written from the perspective of a believer.

Singh, R. (1992) *Immigrants to Citizens: the Sikh Community in Bradford* the Race Relations Research Unit, June, 84pp. The deputy chairman of the Commission for Racial Equality reflects on the changes that have occurred within the Sikh community during the last 20 years. Although the focus of the study is on Bradford, many of the issues covered are pertinent to Sikh communities in various parts of Britain.

Tatla, D.S. and Nesbitt, E. N. (1987) *Sikhs in Britain* Centre for Research in Ethnic Relations, 79pp. Brings together books, reports, theses, scholarly articles

and some audiovisual materials relating to the Sikh community in Britain.

2.8 Buddhism

Morgan, P. (1987) *Buddhism* B T Batsford, 72pp. An A-Z of the main terms and concepts of Buddhism. Illustrated with photographs, this guide provides useful background information to more descriptive and in depth material on Buddhism.

2.9 Hindu groups

Bahree, P. (1984) *Hinduism* Batsford Academic and Educational, 72pp. An A-Z dictionary of the basic concepts, beliefs and rituals of Hinduism. Also covers subjects of general interest such as festivals and marriages. Useful as reference material.

Burghart, R. (ed.) (1987) *Hinduism: the perpetuation of religion in an alien cultural milieu* Tavistock, 290pp. These essays by a wide range of authors examine how Hinduism has perpetuated itself in the West. They cover the rituals of motherhood among Gujarati women, Hindu temples in Britain, marriage and Hare Krishna and Swaminarayan movements. Has a useful bibliography on Hinduism in Britain.

Knott, K. (1986) *Hinduism in Leeds: a study of religious practice in the Indian Hindu community and in Hindu-related,* Community Religions Project, Department of Theology and Religious Studies, University of Leeds, 334pp. Based on field work during 1977-80, this book describes the nature of some aspects of Hinduism in Leeds, outlines population statistics of the Gujarati and Punjabi population in Leeds, and discusses issues around individual and group identity. The book describes the beliefs and practices of Indian-Hindus and Hindu-related groups in the City, religious practices in the Leeds temple, attitudes of temple leaders, and two regular temple services. Includes a useful glossary and bibliography.

Parekh, B. (1994) 'Some Reflections on the Hindu Diaspora' in *New Community,* Volume 20, No. 4, July. Explores the nature, origins and forms of adjustment of the Hindu diaspora. Describes how Hindus in different countries have adapted and reinterpreted their culture in different ways.

Vertovec, S. (1992) 'Community and congregation in London Hindu temples: divergent trends' in *New Community* Volume 18, No. 2, January, pp. 251-264. An

examination of the role played by the temple among three different groups of Hindus in London.

Vertovec, S. (ed.) *Aspects of the South Asian Diaspora* Oxford University Press, 197pp. Articles in this volume explore the varied aspects of overseas South Asian social and cultural development, religious belief and practice and ethnicity in Australia, Netherlands, East Africa and Great Britain. The three most relevant articles are: 'The East African Sikh Diaspora: the British case' by Parminder Bhachu; 'Bound to change? The religions of South Asians in Britain' by Kim Knott; and 'The making of a Pakistani community leader' by Alison Shaw.

2.10 Rastafarians

Barrert, L. (1977) *The Rastafarians: the dreadlocks of Jamaica* Heinemann, 257 pp. This study traces the emergence and development of Rastafarianism in the Jamaican community and its early impact on the Western world.

Campbell, H. (1985) *Rasta And Resistance: from Marcus Garvey to Walter Rodney* Hansib Publishing, 234pp. This is a study of the Rastafarian movement, from its evolution in Jamaica to its presence in Britain. It traces the cultural, political and spiritual sources of this movement, linking its roots to the resistance of oppression.

Cashmore, E. (1979) *Rastaman* Allen and Unwin, 263pp. This well-documented study of Rastafarianism traces the development of the movement in Jamaican society and its impact on British society. Based on interviews and discussions with Rastafarians, it provides a rich tapestry of the cultural, religious and political dimensions of this movement.

Garrison, L. (1979) *Black Youth, Rastafarianism and the Identity Crisis in Britain* Afro-Caribbean Education Research Project, 54pp. Set against the background of hardship, social stress and racial prejudices causing great injury to the dignity and pride of young Afro-Caribbeans in the 1950s and 1960s, Len Garrison examines the rediscovery of Rastafarianism and its relevance to young black people.

Hebdidge, D. (1978) *Reggae, Rastas and Rudies: style and the subversion of form* Occasional Paper, Centre for Contemporary Cultural Studies, University of Birmingham, 30pp. Analyses the Rastafarian movement as a sub-culture which was able to transpose religion, language, music and style while resisting

penetration from white groups and at the same time to enable a highly critical analysis of society.

Lee, B. M. (1980) *Rastafari: the new creation* Jamaica Media Productions, 136-138 New Cavendish Street, London Wl, 66pp. A sympathetic portrayal of Rastafarianism, its cultural and religious practices.

Miles, R. (1978) *Between Two Cultures: the case of Rastafarianism*, SSRC Research Unit on Ethnic Relations, Working Papers on Ethnic Relations No. 10, 34pp. Examines the origins of Rastafarianism in Jamaica and in the British context. Makes a distinction between Rastafarianism as a religious doctrine and as a symbolic movement of protest among many black youth in the UK.

Minority Rights Group (1984) *The Rastafarians* Report No 64, 379 Brixton Road, London SW9 7DE, 11pp. Traces the development of Rasta from its original setting in Jamaica to the inner cities of the UK. It shows why many young black people have so often turned to Rastafarianism. A valuable summary for social and community workers and others interested in Rastafarian philosophy and practice.

Morrish, I. (1982) *Obeah, Christ and Rastaman: Jamaica and its religion* James Clarke, 122pp. Well-documented and scholarly book which places the Rastafarian movement through the religion of African slaves, early Christianity and social and political conditions in Jamaica. Includes chapters on Christian denominations and religion in Jamaica.

Owen, J. (1979) *Dread: The Rastafarians of Jamaica* Heinemann Books, 282pp. Reverend Father Joseph Owens describes with considerable sympathy the religious and cultural contours of the Rastafarian movement in Jamaica.

Plummer, J. (1979) *Movement of Jah People: the growth of Rastafarianism* Press Gang 72pp. Explains the origins and development of Rastafarianism as a way of developing a distinctive black cultural and identity. Includes sections on the impact of its music in popular culture, the movement's conflict with the law and authority and thoughts on its future in Britain.

Tyrona, B. (1978) *Rastafarianism, Reggae and Racism* National Association for Multiracial Education, 20pp. Analyses the impact of the Rastafarian movement on black youth in Britain.

Williams, K. M. (1981) *The Rastafarians* Ward Lock Educational, 64pp. A straight-forward summary of Rastafarian religious and moral beliefs and practices.

2.11 Women

Brah, A. (1993) '"Race" and "culture" in the gendering of labour markets: South Asian young women and the labour market' in *New Community*, Volume 19, No. 3, April pp. 441-458. Based on in-depth interviews with young Muslim women of Pakistani origin as well as group interviews, this article examines the position of these women in the labour market and women themselves view issues concerning paid work.

Hasnain, T. (1983) *Female and Muslim: Double jeopardy?* Centre for the Study of Islam and Christian-Muslim Relations, 26pp. A collection of short articles on Muslim women and equality.

Mirza, K. (1989) *The Silent Cry: Second generation Bradford Muslim women speak* Centre for the Study of Islam and Christian-Muslim Relations, 32pp. Interviews with young Muslim women about their perception of Islam, views of marriage, freedom, Pakistan and other issues.

Sahgal, G. and Yuval-Davis, N. (eds.) (1992) *Refusing Holy Orders: women and fundamentalism in Britain* Virago, 244pp. A collection of articles examining the way women affect and are affected by the rise of religious movements. Authors writing about a wide range of religious communities – Hindu, Christian, Muslim and Jewish – examine how the appeal to culture, religious faith and tradition are used to exert control over the lives of women within the family. Authors include Yasmin Ali on 'Muslim Women and the Politics of Ethnicity and Culture in Northern England' and Elaine Foster on 'Women and the inverted pyramid of the black churches in Britain'.

Sharifi, R. (1985) *Interviews with Young Muslim Women of Pakistani Origin* Centre for the Study of Islam and Christian-Muslim Relations, 48pp. Interviews with young women about their views of dress, marriage, school and racial tension.

The Spring 1991 issue (No. 37) of *Feminist Review* devoted a special feature to 'Women, Religion and Dissent'. The relevant articles are: 'The question for National identity: women, Islam and the state in Bangladesh' by Naila Kabeer;

'Washing our linen: one year of women against fundamentalism' by Clara Connolly; and 'Born against Moon' by Janet McCrickard.

PART 3: BIBLIOGRAPHY ON SOCIAL WORK AND RELIGION

3.1 General sources on social work and religion

CCETSW (1991-1993) *Antiracist Social Work Education* series from the Northern Curriculum Development Project contains seven publications written by various authors. They are:

Patel, N. *et al.* (1991) *Setting the Context for Change* (core text) 193 pp;
Gambe D., Gomes, J., Kapur, V., Rangel, M., Stubbs, P. (1992) *Improving Practice with Children and Families* 102 pp;
Ahmad-Aziz, A., Froggatt, A., Richardson, I., Whittaker, T., Leung, T. (1992) *Improving Practice with Elders* 106 pp;
Clarke, P., Harrison, M., Patel, K., Shah, M., Varley, M., Zack-Williams, T. (1993) *Improving Mental Health Practice* 226 pp;
Bano, A., Crosskill, D., Patel, R., Rashman, L., Shah, R. (1993) *Improving Practice with People with Learning Disabilities* 96 pp;
de Gale, H., Hanlon, P., Hubbard, M., Morgan, S., with Denney, D. (1993) *Improving Practice in the Criminal Justice System* 110 pp. and
Humphries, B., Pankhania-Wimmer, H., Seale, A., Stokes, I. (1993) *Improving Practice Teaching, and Learning* 96 pp.

These publications contain various case studies, resource materials and training exercises. Some material focuses directly on religious considerations and implications for social work practice. Other examples give further thought to the multi-dimensional nature of race, and racism in contemporary social work in Britain.

Cheetham, J. (ed.) (1982) *Social Work and Ethnicity* George Allen & Unwin, 244pp. A text book designed to prepare students, administrators and practitioners to think about and work with ethnic minorities. Most chapters discuss ethnicity, race and racism in relation to minority communities. A few discuss briefly the way religion may affect issues. The chapters on client groups in particular touch on the dilemmas raised when the religious background of ethnic minority clients is raised. Particularly interesting are chapters 5 and 10 which place some emphasis on the problem raised by religious background.

Cheetham, J., James, W., Loney, M., Mayor, B. and Prescott, W. (eds.) (1981)
Social & Community Work in a Multi-Racial Society Harper and Row, 316pp.
Contributors to this book examine issues surrounding service provision as well
as the skills and qualities needed to work in multiracial, multicultural areas.
Most of the articles are concerned with ethnicity and racism although some point
to the importance of religious beliefs and different degrees of religiosity among
groups and individuals.

Coombe, V. and Little, A. (eds.) (1986) *Race and Social Work: a guide to training*
Tavistock Publications, 233pp. Designed primarily for trainers, but also helpful for
students and practitioners, this book provides articles and material to inform
discussions of a range of topics for use in in-service training to help social
workers respond more effectively to the needs of multiracial areas. Most of the
articles are concerned with ethnicity and racism, but a number focus helpfully on
religious identity and beliefs. In particular, chapter 4 by Alix Henly provides
useful material on the religious backgrounds of people of South Asian origin in
Britain. She gives a helpful guide to beliefs and practices under Hinduism,
Sikhism and Islam. In chapter 5, Mohammad Anwar writes about a survey of
young South Asians and their parents carried out by the CRE which shows both
groups to be strongly attached to their religions and culture.

Ely, P. and Denney, D. (1987) *Social Work in a Multi-Racial Society* Gower 231pp. In
this book on the development of antiracist social work policy and practice,
religion is described as a key aspect of the background of ethnic minority
communities which informs discussions on marriages, family relationships and
community systems. Useful as a background publication.

Henderson, P., Jones, D. and Thomas, D. N. (1980) *The Boundaries of Change in
Community Work* George Allen & Unwin 243pp. A mixture of theory, practice and
analysis, this book explores issues facing community work practitioners. An
article by Ismail A. Lambat 'Community work with an Asian community' describes
his work among Indian Muslims of Batley in West Yorkshire.

Khan, V. S. (1979) *Minority Families in Britain: support and stress* Macmillan, 203pp.
This early collection of articles explores the types of stress experienced by
minorities as a result of migration and the settlement process and the systems of
support available to them from within communities and from statutory services.
A chapter by Roger Ballard on ethnic minorities and social services examines

how practitioners can begin to adjust to issues of cultural, religious and ethnic differences between themselves and their clients. A chapter by Verity Khan illustrates how ideas of stress and support can have different meanings in different communities and change over time. Phillip Rack's chapter on Asians and the psychiatric services argues that improvement in services can only be achieved by efforts to understand the background of patients and by the reassessment of diagnostic categories and methods of treatment.

Miles, M. (1995) 'Disability in an Eastern Religious Context: historical perspectives' in *Disability and Society* Volume 10, No. 1. pp. 45-69. Discusses viewpoints and attitudes on disability in Hinduism, Buddhism and Islam primarily in the Indian context.

Ohri, A. Manning, B. and Curno, P. (1982) *Community work and Racism* Routledge & Kegan Paul, 188pp. This collection of articles considers the response of community work to racism. Mike Phillips on the Afro-Caribbean community and Tuku Mukherjee on the Sikh community argue that religious beliefs are central to community experience and organisation.

Various authors (1988) 'Religion and social care' in *Community Care* Inside Supplement, 26 May 7pp. Various articles about the influence of the Judeo-Christian tradition on social service provision. Looks particularly at the influence of religion on statutory social work practice and explores the relationship between the religious voluntary bodies and social services departments. Article 1 examines the work of the Jewish Welfare Board in Leeds. Article 2 considers the role of faith in the provision of care in religious voluntary organisations. Article 3 looks at women's role in church social care. Article 4 describes how a model of social caring developed in the United States is now being taken up in Britain. Article 5 looks at the work of People and Churches Together (PACT), a self-help organisation set up 10 years ago by the United Reform Church with the aim of helping to relieve poverty.

Various authors (1988) 'Cultures of care' in *Community Care* Inside Supplement, 26 July, 7pp. Five articles explore welfare issues from the perspective of different ethnic minority communities in Britain. Article 1 looks at the work of the Islamic Resource centre in Birmingham and the lack of services specifically for Muslim communities. Article 2 on services for elderly South Asian people considers the experience and needs of different religious groups. Article 3 looks at the success

behind the London Borough of Waltham Forest Social Services Department's drive to recruit Asian foster carers. Article 4 looks at experiences of Vietnamese refugees. Article 5 considers the welfare needs of Sikhs in Britain.

Waters, H. (1993) *Resource Directory on 'Race' and Racism in Social Work* London: Institute of Race Relations

3.2 Children and families

Barn, R. (1993) *Black Children in the Public Care System* Batsford in association with British Agencies for Adoption and Fostering, 148pp. Examines the experience of black children in the area of public care. Using evidence gathered from 500 case histories, the author reveals how race and racism affects the decisions made by social workers in the care careers of children. A section on Asian and other minority children reveals how social workers are blind to the importance of religion in the background of children.

Bradford, J. (1995) *Caring for the Whole Child: a holistic approach to spirituality* London: The Children's Society 88pp. This book was written in response to the Children Act 1989 on the needs of children in relation to religion and spiritual concerns The author regards human, devotional and practical spirituality as "fundamental to the overall well-being of every child. The need for faith communities to be supportive to those concerned with child welfare, as well as to *all* children and young people themselves, is reinforced" (cover page). The book provides a framework for understanding and assisting spiritual well-being of children with some practical ideas and implications for social work.

Davis, H. and Choudhry, P. A. (1988) 'Helping Bangladeshi Families: Tower Hamlets parent adviser scheme' in *Mental Handicap* Volume 16, June, pp. 48-51. Using a case example, this article describes the work of a parent adviser who was trained in counselling and child management skills before working with a small number of families. The success of work depended to a large extent on the ability to communicate well with the families but also in being able to respect their cultural, religious and economic circumstances.

Ellahi, R. and Hatfield, C. (1992) 'Research into the needs of Asian families caring for someone with a mental handicap' in *Mental Handicap* Volume 20, December. Based on a survey of families mainly from Pakistan who live in High

Wycombe caring for someone with a mental handicap. The results highlighted the importance of thinking about cultural issues including diet and single-sex services for young women.

Husain, A. S. (1993) 'A Difference of culture' in *Community Care* 17 June, p. 8. Using a detailed case example, the author explains the importance of religion in assessing the needs of Asian children.

MacDonald, S. (1991) *All Equal Under the Act* Race Equality Unit, London, 137pp. Practical guidance on the implications of the Children Act 1989 for social work with ethnic minority children and families. Each section includes team exercises, putting ideas into action, and further reading.

Messent, P. (1992) 'Working with Bangladeshi Families' in *Journal of Family Therapy* Volume 14, pp. 287-304. Based on his work with Bangladeshi Muslim families in the East End of London, the author suggests that family therapy can be a particularly important form of intervention with Asian families in that their culture and background are emphasised as well as the interconnections between different family members.

Neate, P. (1991) 'Bridging the cultural divide' in *Community Care* 21 November, pp. 12-14. Describes the double role played by ethnic minority social workers who have to explain social work and the law to clients and translate their own culture into the system that has to employ them. Includes an interview with Ruth Fasht, social services director at Norwood Child Care, about Norwood's role as a mediating service between Jewish communities and statutory services.

Rapoport, R. N., Fogarty, M. P. and Rapoport, R. (1982) *Families in Britain* Routledge & Kegan and Paul. A collection of articles which look at British family trends from a historical and current perspective. A chapter on South Asian families examines the major features of family organisation, the underlying issues of religion and culture and changing patterns in relationships. Two chapters on West Indian families deal with family life in the Caribbean and the structural patterns and stress points in the British context. A further chapter considers the historical and current patterns among families of Cypriot background.

Shah, R. (1992) *The Silent Majority: children with disabilities in Asian families* National Children's Bureau. This book looks at services for children with disabilities in Asian

communities. It examines the stereotypes held by service providers, explores parents' awareness of services available to them and their perceptions of the effectiveness of service provision. A useful section is on the distinctive cultural, religious and linguistic backgrounds of various Asian communities.

Walrond-Skinner, S. (1989) 'Spiritual dimensions and religious beliefs in family therapy' in *Journal of Family Therapy*, Volume 11, pp. 47-67. Using Christianity as an example, the author considers the way religion as a system of belief might operate within the family and how the recovery of the spiritual dimension may be helpful in the field of family therapy.

3.3 Elderly people

Jackson, H. and Field, S. (1989) *Race, Community Groups and Service Delivery* Home Office Research Study No. 113, HMSO, 61pp. Presents the findings of a household survey comparing the use of voluntary sector services by whites and Gujarati Asians, largely Hindus. The respondents were asked about their use of child care and elderly services, advice and leisure facilities. The report describes how Asians received fewer services than whites and explores the various factors behind the pattern of low use.

Moledina, S. (1987) *Great Expectations: a review of services for Asian elders in Brent* Age Concern Brent, 120 Craven Park Road, London NW10 8QD, 48pp. A study of statutory and voluntary Asian elderly services in Brent. The author asks why services are not being used by this group and recommends ways of making services more accessible to elderly people from ethnic minorities. Provides a detailed profile of the different communities, highlighting differences in language, family structure, religious observances, diet, etc.

Norman, A. (1985) *Triple Jeopardy: growing old in a second homeland* Centre for Policy on Ageing, 180pp. Argues that ethnic minority elders face a triple jeopardy, i.e. they are at risk because of old age and racial discrimination and because of their lack of access to health and social services. Outlines the statistical, cultural and religious background of minority elderly groups, their needs and issues. Includes sections on housing, health, voluntary day centre provision and other services.

Social Policy Committee of the Board for Social Responsibility (1990) *Ageing* Church House Publishing, 151pp. This report looks at current social trends,

policies affecting older people and the needs of those who care for relatives and friends. Its main emphasis is on how the Christian faith can help us make sense of changes involved in growing old. It discusses, although very briefly, the particular issues facing minority ethnic elderly people. It is a useful model for work on the religious and spiritual needs of the different ethnic minority elderly groups.

Squires, A. (ed.) (1991) *Multicultural Health Care and Rehabilitation of Older People* Edward Arnold, 210pp. Contributors from a variety of professional backgrounds address the particular needs of elders from ethnic minorities. Many of the articles deal at great length with the way religion and culture affects the contexts in which ethnic minority elderly services are planned. Authors include John Young and James George on 'The history of migration to the United Kingdom', and Bashir Qureshi on 'Traditions of ethnic minority groups'. The final section includes a summary and recommendations, useful addresses and further reading. The articles deal with issues clearly and comprehensively.

3.4 Bereavement

Bhaduri, R. (1990) 'Crossing the divide', in *Social Work Today* 29 March, p.28. A transcultural approach to bereavement counselling, placing emphasis on spiritual values which, the author argues, could help social workers cope with bereaved clients.

Black, J. (1987) 'Broaden your mind about death and bereavement in certain ethnic groups in Britain' in *British Medical Journal* Volume 295, No. 6597, 29 August, pp. 536-539. The religious beliefs and needs of a dying patient and relatives from the three main religions of the Indian sub-continent - Hinduism, Sikhism and Islam.

ANTIRACIST SOCIAL WORK EDUCATION SERIES

This widely acclaimed series was produced as part of CCETSW's Curriculum Development Project. Each title is available separately or at a discount rate for the complete set, comprising the initial core text and six training manuals.

1. Setting the Context for Change
Naina Patel and others
Gives a comprehensive and critical analysis of the state of racism, antiracism and Black struggles, with a focus on social work and social work education in Britain.
1991   0 904488 79 9   193 pages

2. Improving Practice with Children and Families
David Gambe, Jenny Gomes, Vijay Kapur, Moira Rangel and Paul Stubbs
Includes the implementation of the Children Act 1989 in a discussion of child care issues.
1992   1 85719 006 8   102 pages

3. Improving Practice with Elders
Arshi Ahmad-Aziz, Alison Froggatt, Ian Richardson, Terri Whittaker and Tim Leung
Identifies key issues in the law, the organisational context and in assessment, decision making and counselling skills.
1992   0 904488 99 3   106 pages

4. Improving Mental Health Practice
Pam Clarke, Mary Harrison, Kamlesh Patel, Mani Shah, Mary Varley and Tunde Zack-Williams
Guidelines to develop and consolidate sound mental health practice and assess progress.
1993   1 85719 021 1   226 pages

5. Improving Practice with People with Learning Disabilities
Aktar Bano, Daryl Crosskill, Rafiq Patel, Lyndsay Rashman and Robina Shah
A clear, antiracist perspective for training in the field, this looks at the connection between race and underachievement in education.
1993   1 85719 049 1   96 pages

6. Improving Practice in the Criminal Justice System
Hamilton de Gale, Peter Hanlon, Michael Hubbard, Steve Morgan with David Denney
For practising and prospective probation officers and their tutors, this manual aims to provide the means to develop sound antiracist practice.
1993   1 85719 053 X   110 pages

7. Improving Practice Teaching and Learning
Beth Humphries, Harsa Pankhania-Wimmer, Alex Seale and Idris Stokes
Designed to help programme providers establish antiracist policies and practice in education and training.
1993   1 85719 032 7   96 pages

Also available from CCETSW

Children, Spirituality and Religion: a training pack
edited and compiled by Margaret Crompton
Complementary to *Visions of Reality*, this comprehensive training resource is designed to help social work and social care practitioners understand the religious and spiritual aspects of their work with children and young people. The materials are drawn from a variety of sources and represent a wide range of religions and belief including:

- Buddhism
- Christianity
- Hinduism
- Islam
- Judaism
- Rastafarianism
- Sikhism
- Humanism

Produced in a spiral-bound format for ease of access, subject areas covered by the pack include: relevant legislation and children's rights; ideas about spiritual development; an introduction to the beliefs and observances of the religions included; implications for social work; and suggestions for communicating with children.
1996   1 85719 166 8   270 pages

Perspectives on Discrimination and Social Work in Northern Ireland
Faith Gibson, Gill Michael and Dorothy Wilson
Whilst the focus of this training pack is primarily on understanding religious discrimination and its relevance to social work in Northern Ireland, the material can be used and discussed in a variety of other contexts.

Designed for social work tutors and practice teachers to use with students, the pack is divided into three main areas:
● materials on human rights from both European and global perspectives;
● a wide range of individual and group exercises, including comparisons of news coverage;
● and detailed research on religious discrimination in Northern Ireland.
1994   1 85719 083 1   226 pages

Reflections: views of disabled people on their lives and community care
edited by Nasa Begum, Mildrette Hill and Andy Stevens
"We use this book" writes Nasa Begum, "to reflect on our lives and start a dialogue with those of you who have the power to support and empower other Black Disabled people either directly through social work practice, or indirectly through policy and practice formulation."
1994   1 85719 0815   200 pages

For information on prices or availability, or for a full list of CCETSW publications, or to place an order please contact:

Mail Order Unit
CCETSW, Derbyshire House, St Chad's Street, London WC1H 8AD
Tel: 0171 278 2455   Fax: 0171 278 2934

Information Service
CCETSW, 78-80 George Street, Edinburgh EH2 3BU
Tel: 0131 220 0093   Fax: 0131 220 6717

Information Service
CCETSW, 6 Malone Road, Belfast BT9 5BN
Tel: 01232 665390   Fax: 01232 669469

Information Service
CCETSW, South Gate House, Wood Street, Cardiff CF1 1EW
Tel: 01222 226257   Fax: 01222 384764